REINVENTED

Scripture quotations taken from the (NASB®) New American Standard Bible®, Copyright © 1960, 1971, 1977, 1995, 2020 by The Lockman Foundation. Used by permission. All rights reserved. lockman.org

Scripture quotations taken from the Holy Bible: Easy-to-Read Version™ © 2006 by Bible League International. Used by permission.

Print ISBN: 979-8-9881581-9-6

Digital ISBN: 979-8-9903602-0-4

Audio ISBN: 979-8-9903602-1-1

LCCN: 2024907272

Cover and Interior Design by Nelly Murariu at PixBeeDesigns.com

Manuscript Edits by Ashton Renshaw, Raejan Noh, and Market Refined Media, LLC

Printed in the United States of America

First Edition: May 2024

REINVENTED

My Journey of Addiction
and
Redemption

MIKE CINELLI

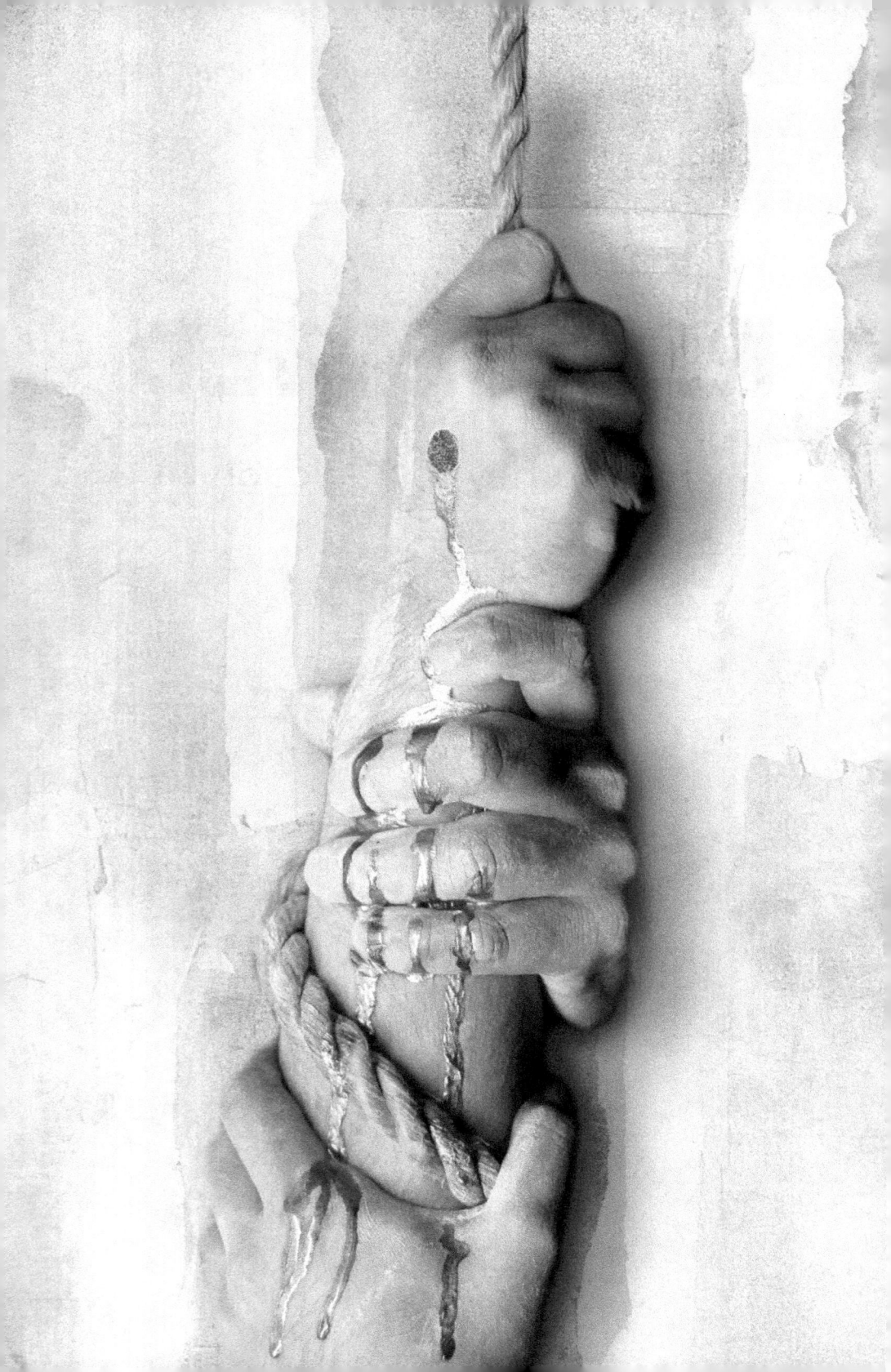

DEDICATION

Mom

I have been blessed by your prayers, your wisdom, and your dependence upon the Holy Spirit.

Aunt Kathy

Thank you for the countless hours you spent helping me polish this book.

CONTENTS

FOREWORD

Helplessness is your constant companion. Fear hovers like a cloud and follows you all day, intent on devouring you. Hope sparks and is then dashed to the depths of your heart—over and over again.

Michael Cinelli is my son. The cycle in and out of hope and help-lessness is his story—and the story of all of us who love him.

In the following pages, you will read the bad, the ugly, and the good. I've been a pastor for many years, but it's my own son's story that has taken me on a journey into a world of addiction and recovery I never imagined I would experience.

Along the way, I've met wonderful people traveling the same path. They helped me to start a recovery outreach where hundreds have found help and hope.

I am so proud of my son for sharing his story of suffering and mayhem. His desire, and mine, is that these chapters will offer hope and encouragement for the hurting addict and their loved ones. This story is a testament to the fact that recovery *is* possible.

God is faithful, and I am thankful to Him that my son is recovering, enjoying a loving marriage, and leading a successful business. He continues to be a support in the recovery world, the church, and the community.

Michael and Ivette, thank you for your testimony. May it widely proclaim the hope and help you have found in the God Who never gives up on anyone.

Pastor Mario Cinelli

PROLOGUE

It wasn't a noise that woke me. It was a silence so consuming it felt like a weight was pressing on my back.

Where am I?

I struggled to regain consciousness through the dense fog in my head. The putrid odors of gas, oil, and asphalt lingered in my nostrils. Gradually, a splinter of light began to seep in as I fought to open my swollen eyes. I groaned with pain when I tried to move—my body immediately notified me that I hadn't slept on a soft mattress last night. I could barely lift my head from the concrete curb pillow where my cheek was still a little stuck. I rubbed my face and bits of gravel rolled off.

Gotta be some imprint. Okay, so I managed one lucid thought.

The fact was, I hadn't slept on a soft mattress for a long time. For several weeks, my home was in the alley behind a strip mall. My only furnishings were a smelly, over-full dumpster and a disintegrating remnant of a mattress. Sheets of cardboard proved insufficient protection from the rusted metal springs. Slabs of Styrofoam almost kept the rain off. But last night, one of the restaurant owners had doused my home with gallons of vinegar. I knew I wouldn't be sleeping there anymore. *So what? Not my first eviction.*

Memories of last night crept back in sporadic bursts.

No more back-alley home. No place to go. Wandering the streets. Grabbing a backpack from a random parked car some clown had left unlocked. Sprinklers showering me with bone-chilling spray. Drugs. Xanax.

How many did I take? Two? Three? More? A powdery after-taste lingered in the back of my throat. I needed water.

"Probably three." The muffled voice startled me until I realized that it had come from my own mouth. I didn't remember passing out on the curb. Gasping and groaning, I tried to get up. The agonizing pain in my back and side was nearly unbearable. Maneuvering into an almost-sitting position took several minutes.

I tried to check out my surroundings. My eyes refused to focus. They finally settled on a streetlight some yards away. I could hear traffic noises in the distance. I needed to go before I was discovered. Standing upright was another long battle. Carefully, I tested my weight on each shaky leg. As I struggled to straighten my back, a flash of purple caught my eye. I looked down and saw my entire body was covered in a too-small clown costume, complete with frilly ruffled sleeves and fluffy purple button balls.

"Wha . . . ?" More memories arose through the haze. The sprinklers! I had passed out on the grass. I had crawled to the curb to escape the icy sprinkler spray and grabbed the first item of clothing I could find to ward off the biting cold. What a joke. The owner of the parked car really was a clown.

This had been my life for several weeks. Embracing any emotion was a sensation from somewhere in the past. That was the purpose of the drugs, right? Yet, in that moment, I felt a soul-crushing stirring of shame in the depths of my being. I guessed I was lucky to be drug-numbed. Outside of my present state, I would have been wholly incapacitated by the humiliation.

Huh. Multi-colored humiliation.

Unsteadily, I tipped back my head and gazed up into the sky. I only heard the sound of my ragged breathing. The streetlight blinked off, as if snuffed out by the early morning light.

"What am I even doing here?" The words came out in a moan, a result of my utter misery. They landed on no one's ears. Unless . . .

God?

I was pretty sure I had burned all the bridges between us. Still, I grasped for a fragment of promised hope. If all those Sunday School Bible stories were true, if all those prayers were actually heard by a God Who loves—Who cares—then maybe those bridges weren't burned after all. I was a pastor's kid, for crying out loud. How did that good little boy even get *here*? A ruined, dejected, broken man who slept on a curb on an abandoned street and woke up in a drugged stupor all alone, dressed in a ridiculous clown costume.

This is not the beginning of the story. And the ending is still being written. It's a hard story. Some of the questions may never be answered on this side of heaven.

But it's a story that needs to be told.

CHAPTER 1

CANCER!

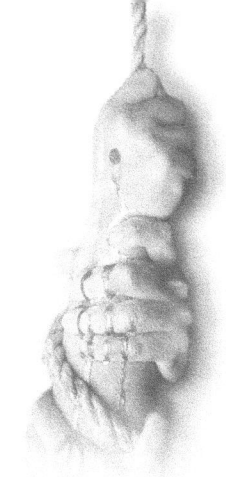

"Mom? Mommy?"

Alone in the dark, I couldn't determine where I was. My pajamas stuck to my hot, sweaty skin. Struggling to untangle from the damp sheets and the terror gripping my heart, I felt soft hands touch my shoulders. *Auntie*. I was in my cousins' bedroom.

"You're okay, honey. You're safe. You were having a nightmare." The face looming above me was caring and looked concerned. It wasn't Mommy. Loving arms held me tight as I sobbed inconsolably. I really needed my mother.

Being separated from her for a whole month was more than my four-year-old heart could bear. It seemed like an eternity. It felt like abandonment. I cried until fatigue claimed me and I relaxed into my aunt's embrace.

My mom had cancer. She had been diagnosed with lung cancer some weeks ago. Dad had taken her to a clinic in New York City for her treatments. My ears heard the information, but truly understanding it wasn't possible. Doctors fix people.

What was taking so long?

My mom and dad were always described as good people and super parents. They had met at one of those Tupperware home parties. Dad wasn't really in need of plastic bowls with snap-lock lids. He was actually focused on the petite blonde examining the autumn gold canister set. He had first noticed her at church, and he attended the party because he heard that she would be there. After enduring the twenty-minute product demonstration, he resisted the temptation to purchase the sandwich storage set just to be polite. Instead, he asked the blonde if she would be interested in seeing him again. She agreed.

Some months later, my dad—a handsome, hard-working Italian from a New York City borough—and my mom—a sweet, pretty farmer's daughter from a small town in Vermont—stood before God, their family, and their friends and pledged to love one another until death should part them.

It was a bright summer day in June.

According to my parents, I was a miracle. No matter how many times Dad repeated the story, I never got tired of hearing it:

> As soon as we were married, we wanted to start a family. It just wasn't happening. It was a bit depressing that we had tried for a few years with no success. We questioned God. One evening at a church service, the pastor stopped talking in the middle of his sermon. He said he felt that there were two couples in the audience who wanted to have children, but hadn't been able to. We, along with the other couple, hesitantly went to the front. The pastor prayed and the presence of the Lord was so strong that we could not stand up. We were on the floor, embarrassed, but could not move for several minutes. We left there not quite sure what to think. A few months later, we were expecting. You are our miracle!

I was to be Mom and Dad's only child.

During her first doctor's visit after my birth, they discovered that Mom had cervical cancer, so they quickly performed surgery to remove the tumor. I spent several of my earliest weeks in the care of my mom's best friend. The hysterectomy determined we would remain a family of three.

My parents were devoted to me. They were kind and patient, and they enveloped me in love beyond measure. My childhood world had felt good and normal.

When my parents returned from the New York clinic, the news was not encouraging. The treatments hadn't produced positive results. The prognosis was less than promising.

Finally back together with my parents, I was excited to get dressed up on Sunday and go to church with them. But on that Sunday, Dad came out of the bedroom alone.

"Isn't Mom coming?"

"Not today. She isn't feeling well."

He and I got into the car, just the two of us, and headed off to church. And so began a lonely pattern that would continue over the next two-plus years.

One of those Sundays, as I headed for my class, I ran into a lady who must have known my mom. She knelt to my eye level. The news that Mom was not doing well was a widespread story by now. The woman grasped my shoulders. Her serious face was too close to mine. Her breath was pure peppermint. I thought about the bowl of candy on the desk in the lobby. I wanted to turn away from her pungent perfume, but I felt duty-bound not to move.

"Michael, I had a dream about your mom. If we pray hard and have enough faith, she will be healed!" Her fingers tightened on my little shoulders as she spoke with determination.

The words pierced my fragile soul. I wanted to believe them so much that it hurt. It was a sizable and weighty task assigned to such a small, innocent boy, but my heart clung to this morsel of hope. For as long as I could remember, I had been singing songs about God's mighty power. My dad was a pastor. He must have a special connection with God, right? I knew I mustn't fail to pray every night.

"Dear Jesus, please heal my mommy."

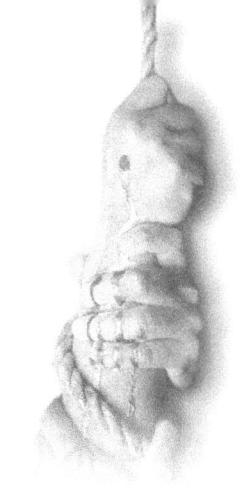

CHAPTER 2

SAD GOODBYES

My eyes opened to rays of sunlight beaming through the bedroom window. Last night, I had fallen asleep alone in my parents' bed. I was still alone. Dad must have spent the night in the hospital with Mom. Once, this bed had been my refuge—a safe place to cuddle between Mom and Dad after a bad dream. Dad and I had knelt beside this bed many times, praying for Mom again and again while she was in the hospital. It had never been a lonely place, but it was today. I thought about spending the whole day just lying right there.

Sitting up, I tried to untwist my favorite red T-shirt from around my back. I must have had a restless night. The shirt still held Mom's scent from the last time we snuggled over a week ago. So far, I had been able to keep it from my grandmother. She seemed to love doing laundry.

Eventually, I decided to move into the living room. I settled on the couch. The inviting sounds and smells of breakfast drifted from the kitchen, though I was pretty sure I couldn't eat. Grammy came in from her cooking with a spatula in her hand. She turned on the television for me and asked if I was hungry.

"Not really. Where's Daddy?"

"He spent the night at the hospital." She turned away.

Did I imagine I saw sadness in her eyes? I turned to the TV. The cartoons were calling for my attention, but my thoughts were on another day.

I had just finished kindergarten and my class had a graduation ceremony. We had caps, gowns, and certificates just like the big high school graduates. Everyone's parents watched us walk across the stage, proudly waving our diplomas. But Mom couldn't go. Disappointment tried to threaten my excitement.

"Look what I got, Mom!" I waved my certificate of graduation as Dad and I entered the hospital room. I was super thrilled that the school had let me wear my cap and gown to the hospital.

"Wow, honey! How exciting!" Her cheeks were swollen and puffy, but I knew I would never forget the smile she gave me. She examined the certificate for a long time. She told me how handsome and grown up I looked in the cap and gown. I sat on the bed with her. We had a great visit.

"I love you." She leaned over and kissed me. She always told me how she loved to kiss my chubby little cheeks. She spoke so softly. I could feel her love.

I leaned my head into her shoulder. "I love you, too, Mommy."

It was the sweetest of moments. The sweetest of goodbyes. No one realized it would be the last time we spoke.

"Grammy, when is Daddy coming home?"

Before she could answer me, the front door opened. My aunt and my dad walked in. Dad walked right by me without a glance. Auntie sat down beside me.

We were in my favorite spot on the couch, right where Mom would read to me. Right where she would sing to me as she rubbed my back. Right where I would gently scratch her itchy scar after the operation that had removed her whole right lung. Right there, my Auntie had to say the words I never wanted to hear. I could hear her talking, but she wasn't making sense. Her words sounded foreign.

No, God was going to heal my mother!

Daddy?!

My mind screamed, but my mouth was unable to form words. How could I grow up without a mother? My seventh birthday was in less than a month. Despair seeped into my little boy heart. My good and normal life was beginning to dissolve into a murky haze.

It was a bright summer day in June.

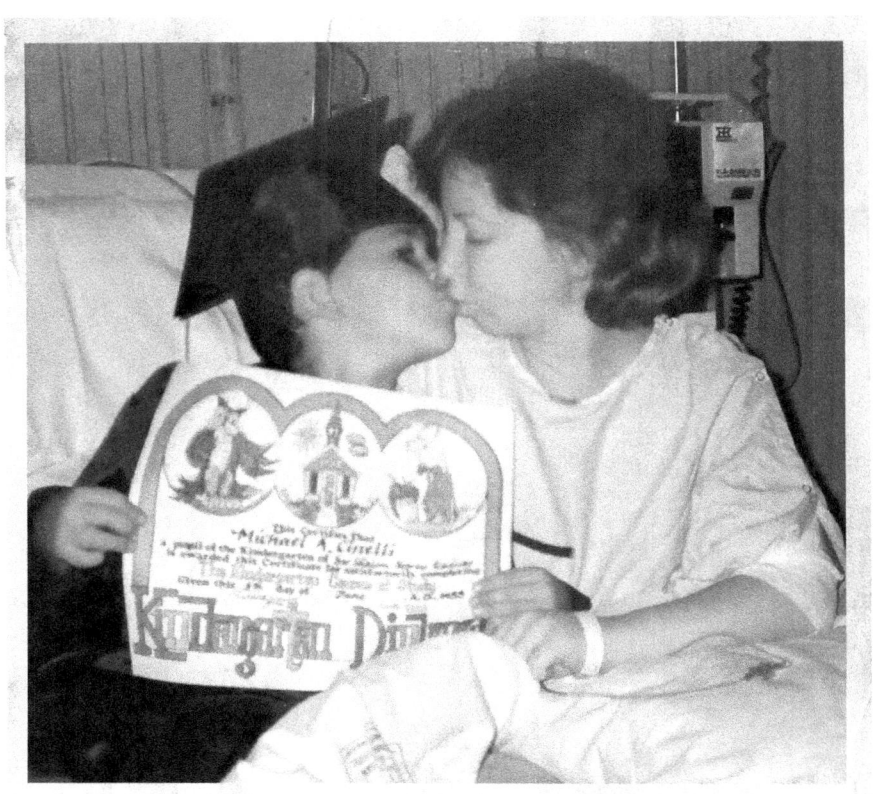

CHAPTER 3

WAITING

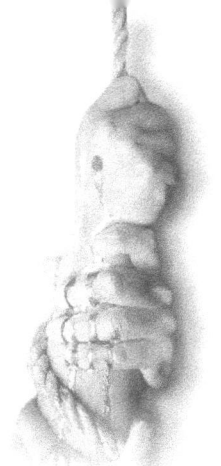

I stood frozen. The low buzz of muted conversations was the only indication that there were other people in the room. There were so many flowers, but I saw nothing except the casket. The rest of the room seemed to dissolve into various shades of green. I was holding my dad's hand. Taking that first step was hard to do. We walked slowly toward my mom. I could almost see my reflection in the casket's smooth side.

Mom lay perfectly still on a bed of creamy, soft satin. Her light brown hair had been neatly arranged around her face. Her eyes were closed, her face relaxed. She could have been sleeping. I wanted to kiss her cheek like she had always kissed mine. Standing on my tiptoes, I could only reach her arm. I didn't ask to be lifted up. My mouth couldn't form words. In silence, I resigned and kissed her arm. I don't think my dad noticed. It was at that moment the enduring notion that no one could see my pain—or desired to meet my need—began to etch itself into my soul.

I stared at Mom. It hurt so much to look at her, but I couldn't rip my eyes away. She wore the emerald green dress I remembered was her favorite. It draped in folds around her tiny body. The cancer had caused her to lose so much weight. I understood that I was here to say goodbye. I would never understand why I had to. I couldn't do it. I was not ready to believe this was final. I felt like my heart had nothing in it. No emotion came up to the surface. The murky haze was all that remained, a fog so thick

I imagined I wouldn't see my hand if I lifted it in front of my face. Perhaps I would never see light again.

Those thoughts were too big for such a small boy.

Someone took my hand and led me to a car. I felt rushed.

Why?

Dad was driving away in another car.

Where could he be going without me?

No one spoke during the car ride. In my mind, I pictured myself seated at a table in front of a large picture window. Looming clouds hovered on the horizon. My elbows rested on the table, my chin in my hands. There I was, waiting. Mom would come home. She would hold me and say she loved me. I decided I would just wait.

The next morning, I lay on the couch in my favorite spot again. I gazed in the direction of the television. Perhaps this normal activity would help me to escape the throbbing agony in my heart.

Everyone was leaving to attend Mom's funeral.

"Are you ready to go?"

I told my dad I did not want to go. I told him I wanted to watch the new dinosaur movie. My cousin could stay with me.

I did stay behind. But the dinosaur movie was no match for the silent suffering that pushed me further into darkness—the darkness I would slowly drown in for the next twenty years. Misery was establishing itself in the very depths of my soul.

That morning, seeds of bitterness and resentment found fertile ground in my young, broken heart. There was nothing my innocent mind could do to ever make sense of all of this. I felt alone. I felt abandoned.

What about those people who had claimed Mom would be healed if we believed strongly enough?

I had tried my best to believe. I had prayed. If there really was a God, it seemed obvious that He was not listening.

Or He simply did not care.

CHAPTER 4

FEELING ALONE

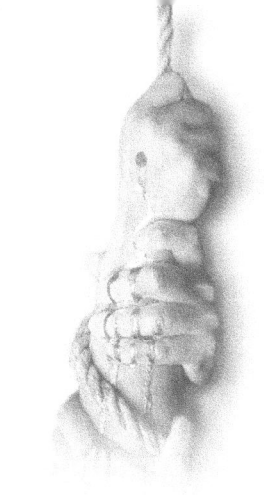

Four long years had passed since Mom had gone to Heaven, but the tender wound of her loss remained unhealed. I was ten years old and was fraught with fear that my dad would also go away. I was so sad, grasping at any morsel of affection or acceptance. My dad was distracted. He must have been hurting also. I had friends, family, birthday parties, and holidays but they didn't matter. Nothing mattered. Even amidst the loving people around me, I felt a crushing sense of loneliness. I felt like no one understood. It was just a few months before my eleventh birthday. I tried to stay strong, but deep down, I was terrified. I couldn't go to sleepovers. I couldn't even take a shower without my dad standing right outside the door. I was afraid someone would take me or take him, and leave me all alone.

Once again, on the same spot on the same couch, I lay considering what had been happening recently. Like a breath of fresh air, a new woman had appeared in our lives. Dad was dating someone, and she was giving me attention. I didn't want to betray my mom. However, I couldn't deny my desperation for love.

Picking at a pilling piece of fabric on the cushion, I quietly resolved to do what I hadn't done since the day I kissed my mom goodbye. I was going to open my heart to this woman. I even began to feel something like love for her. She would sit on the couch with me, not realizing she was in my favorite spot. Her perfume lingered even after she was gone. I could have lain there all day taking in the aroma. I wished it would never end. Hope crept in. Ever so slightly, the fog began to dissipate. I felt like I was rising from the dead.

This woman, Cherie (who would become my stepmom), had moved to Florida from her home state of Virginia. She began attending the church where my family were members—the same church where my mom and dad had met.

The same church where Mom and Dad had received prayer for their miracle son.

The same church where I had been told Mom would be healed if I could just believe.

Could this be something good? Could this mean the grief might go away? Let's see what happens . . . I reluctantly decided.

It wasn't long before my dad proposed. She said yes. Dad sent me with Cherie to help her pick out a wedding ring. I was so excited to be included in this experience. On the way, in the quiet of the car, I began to unravel my thoughts.

Would this woman try to take my mother's place?

Back home, I questioned my dad. "Are you and Cherie going to be together like you and Mom were?"

"Yes, it will be like having someone new to take care of us."

Fear rose and exploded in my mind. *I cannot let that happen!* I silently screamed.

In an act of defiance, I grabbed Dad's car keys and threw them on the roof. The very idea of that woman pushing the memory of Mom away was more than I could manage. And so, it began: the battle between accepting—and refusing to accept—what was happening in my life. I must not and would not betray my mother.

After a short engagement, Dad and Cherie were married. I cycled between feeling thrilled and feeling apprehensive several times each day. Aided by the family trip to Disney World they planned for after the honeymoon, I eventually landed on excitement.

The first night in the hotel, in a room with two queen-sized beds, I asked Cherie if she would sleep in the bed with me.

She agreed. I felt comfortable and content. A typhoon of memories overtook my mind before sleep rescued me. I remembered the nightmares I had when Mom and Dad had to leave me while they were away for her cancer treatments. I recalled waking up alone when Dad had to stay all night at the hospital. I shuddered at the memory of the deep loneliness encompassing me when my aunt had told me Mom was gone. Unstoppable tears accompanied the feelings of abandonment that had become way too familiar.

As morning dawned and sleep faded, I looked around. Cherie was gone! *I knew it. I knew this wouldn't last. She abandoned me too.*

When I looked around the room for any signs of her, I saw that she was in the other bed with my dad. She must have moved during the night. Tears streamed down my cheeks. Anger and fear gripped my throat, and I felt as if I wouldn't be able to take a breath. I crawled under the bed, intending to never come out. No amount of consolation could coax me from behind this wall of pain.

Physically, I did eventually come out from under the bed. Emotionally, I left everything that had been important to me under there. I had done what I swore I would never do. I had betrayed my mother. I had opened my heart to someone else.

She had smashed it. Though this was the unsophisticated reasoning of an eleven-year-old child, it was real enough to send me again into the depths of immense suffering. I had been rendered voiceless. Invalid. A simple fact firmly settled in my heart.

I was on my own.

CHAPTER 5

UPROOTED

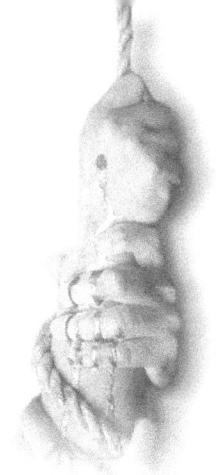

When I was growing up, the homeschooling movement was flourishing. My mom wanted to teach me at home, but when she became ill, my parents had to enroll me in school. I went to a private school for kindergarten, first, and second grade. After Mom died, Dad took me out of the school to try homeschooling. He owned a pool cleaning company, so he could choose his own hours. It worked out well for him to teach me in the mornings and work in the afternoons, while I spent time at my aunt's house with my cousins.

My stepmom took over as my teacher after she and Dad were married. Dad began to talk to me about trying to see Cherie as a "mother figure." He even suggested that it might help if I called her "Mom." I wanted a mother so much, but I just couldn't do it. It felt like I was betraying *my* mom.

One day, when Cherie and I were visiting friends, I was playing with the boys and we were chasing each other through the house. I was picking on the youngest one and he called out to her, "Aren't you going to spank him? You're his mother now."

She answered, a bit too quickly, "I'm not his mother. I can't spank him."

I knew that Dad and Cherie had agreed that he would be the primary disciplinarian. Still, those words rang in my ears. Confusion plagued me. I wanted her to mother me. Yet, I continued to reject her advances and attempts to do that. Now here she was confessing no ownership of the position?

A few days later, I was at my aunt's house again. I tried to articulate my mixed-up emotions about this issue to my aunt.

"Well, Cherie is like your mom now. Maybe you should try calling her 'Mom.'"

Foreboding fear climbed up my spine. My beloved aunt wasn't even on my side. As I sank deeper into my suffering, I had only one thought to hang on to: *At least I still have my dad.*

Fear, pain, guilt, anger, and loneliness were my daily companions. Emotionally, I was frozen at seven years old, sitting in front of that large window and waiting for my mom to come home. To hold me tight. To whisper in my ear that she loved me. To reassure me that she would always protect me. I needed to feel loved.

Desperation has few inhibitions. It can convince you to do things you instinctively know are wrong. I had a pre-teen crush on a girl. I happened to find a poem in a magazine that contained an acronym with the same letters as her name. I copied it and showed it to my dad.

"Look what I wrote." The words spilled out of my mouth. I hadn't meant to lie. However, my need for acceptance and approval, of any kind, overruled my conscience.

"Wow, what a great poem!"

I basked in my dad's genuine pride. In fact, his reaction incited the desire in my heart to eventually write my own poetry. I couldn't wait to give the poem to the object of my affection. But before I could do that, I found out that her family was moving away. She would be gone forever. I decided the poem was worthless. Rejection grew new roots in my soul. Yet, a tiny spark of hope remained. I knew there had to be love somewhere out there—love just for me. I would spend my days looking for it.

"Do we really have to leave here?"

Dad had decided to sell our house. We would buy a new house, and the three of us would begin a new life together. I sat on the floor, looking at the empty walls. The pictures were all packed away. Leaving here would mean leaving my mother. Leaving all the memories of her and of our life with her. The couch where we had shared my favorite spot. Where I had heard the news that she was gone. The coffee table where I stored my favorite game we had played together. I wished we could play Monopoly again.

Sitting there on our empty living room floor, my jumbled thoughts began to race. I saw my mom's face in my mind.

It was a flashback to one day when I had been playing outside with my friends. Mom had opened the door and asked me if I wanted to come inside to spend time with her.

"No!" I had called back. "I want to play with my friends."

Perhaps she knew she was dying then. I was sure I had seen extreme disappointment on her face as she closed the door. Shame and guilt engulfed me.

What was I thinking? I could have spent more time with her. I didn't know she was sick.

I didn't want to leave that house. The pool where we had swum together. The kitchen where we had enjoyed family meals. The bedroom where Mom had tucked me in and sung to me. *How did that song go?* Unexpectedly, I couldn't remember. Sadness took my breath away. It was all moving too fast. Life would be so different.

I am not ready! I am not ready to face the agony of letting go.

I saw myself as powerless and utterly defeated. My soul ached. No one seemed to comprehend the feelings of bitterness and abandonment I lived with every day. My heart was broken, maybe beyond repair.

She can never be replaced! I wanted to scream at everyone.

I felt like I was back standing by the casket, needing to be lifted up. No one saw my need or my pain.

Smack! The large wooden spoon, which had been dedicated as a disciplinary tool, placed its signature on my deep-rooted rejection. I began to cry. My dad hadn't spanked me in a very long time—maybe even years. *Why now?* Thinking back over the day, I realized the correction was for talking back to Cherie.

It was her fault.

She was the reason Dad had taken to spanking me. It wasn't just me and Dad anymore. My stepmother had stolen the only person I had left in this world. I was right about being on my own. Really on my own. An ember of hatred sparked to life. How could I have known it would ultimately grow into raging flames?

Anger beyond containment took over my senses. No one would ever control me again. As my stepmother, Cherie deserved to be shown respect. However, I was determined to fight back. I made a commitment to fight with all my might. From then on, battles were commonplace. Dad was in the middle, always seeming to lean toward her side. The enormity of—what I considered—invalidated pain, the clutching tentacles of immense grief from losing my mother, and the resentment of feeling forced to live a life with which I did not agree had erected a wall around my mind and heart. Tall and thick, the wall allowed neither reason nor wisdom to enter.

I just can't wait to get out of here.

Escaping was my only hope.

CHAPTER 6

INDEPENDENT?

"That's it! We're finished!" I yelled, as if the volume of my voice could make the statement more final. I listened. Silence filled the line. She had hung up. So what? Broken relationships were becoming a habit. But . . . this one was momentous. We were still teenagers. This wasn't just the end of another teenage crush. This one was the one that altered the course of my life. Once, I had been sure someone, somewhere out there, would truly love me. Now, I knew better.

Fiery rage burned through my body and drove my fist through the bedroom wall. Drywall gave way and scattered on the floor in dusty heaps. The picture frame stood its ground and sliced my knuckles. *Huh.* This wasn't the first time I had bloody knuckles. I had been working out my frustrations by punching an old piece of plywood in my backyard for some time now. Temples throbbing, heart hammering my chest, I bolted out the door. The hot, wet Florida summer collided with my anger. I paced, zig-zagging across the driveway. I had to stop this agony.

I knew my friend regularly smoked marijuana. Maybe some weed would do the trick. I made the call. I was sixteen and drove my own truck. In just a matter of minutes, I was getting an education on prepping and packing a bowl.

"The high is better if you inhale and cough," my friend told me.

Great. I need to be oblivious. I placed my finger over the hole in the pipe like my friend told me and inhaled. *Ahhh.* My thoughts began to quiet. I released my breath and coughed, waving away the cloud of smoke I had puffed into my eyes.

I could focus. The pain stopped. Rage and anxiety subsided. I had escaped. I was free! Only the twitching of my muscles occupied my mind. I finally found something that understood me. This was the perfect distraction. No thoughts about how much of a failure I was. No worries about stepmothers or lost relationships. No grief. No cares at all. I wanted to live like this forever.

The decision was made. The corner was turned. I would make it my life's priority to do whatever it took to maintain this state of distraction. I had no idea then what pursuing that kind of distraction would mean. Or what it would cost.

My dad owned an apartment building on the beach. I had heard him talking about one unit being empty.

"Can I move in?"

"I don't know . . . You aren't even eighteen yet."

I felt like I had only a few talents. The art of persuading my father was one I had honed regularly. Using unprincipled techniques was not a problem. Taking advantage of his feelings of sorrow for me would not deter me. I'd do whatever it took.

I knew I could pay the rent. I had a little mobile car detailing business going. To me, earning money meant independence. As a kid, I had worked over the summer for my dad's pool cleaning business because I wanted a stereo system for my room. I loved to work. I loved cleaning pools and detailing cars. I found working and earning my own money satisfying and fulfilling. That summer, I had bought the biggest stereo system with the deepest bass.

With a couple months' rent saved and a determination to do whatever it would take, I moved into the small apartment just before my eighteenth birthday. At last, I could do whatever I wanted without a parent looking over my shoulder. And for the next six months, I did. I had no plans. No direction. My only purpose in life was to find my next escape into oblivion. Slowly, my determination faded to drug-induced indifference. I was living behind a cloud again, just like after my mom died. Only this one was of my own creation, and I didn't feel anything. My detailing business fell apart from a lack of attention. I was scrounging any odd job I could find.

I was dating another girl, and we decided to move in together. A few months later, on a whim, we decided to move again into a bigger place with a roommate. That was not a good decision. We were fighting constantly. I braced myself for another broken heart. Sure enough, one day I returned home from work to find she had packed up her stuff and left.

"I don't care anymore," I said to our now-empty bed.

I resolved that, no matter what, I would never care. Chasing the blackness that chemicals provided was my new obsession. If you're going to do something, you might as well do it right. Go all in. It seemed like people were always going to fail me. The consequences of doing drugs could be scary, maybe dangerous, but while I was doing them, the results were always predictable. Not like people. Drugs would not disappoint me.

"Hey, Mike, I'm having some people over. Want to hang out with us?"

My roommate knew lots of people and always loved to throw a party. At the party that night, I met a kindred spirit.

"You want to smoke?" he offered.

"Absolutely!" I hadn't smoked weed in a while. I had graduated to ecstasy a few months ago. I was in love with the chemicals and fell for everything I tried. Addicts love the consistency of the expectation. Emotions created tornadoes of disruption and turmoil. I spent all my energy barely keeping myself together. But with chemicals, I had something I could turn to. The turmoil was here to stay. At this point, there was no running from it. My only option was burying it in oblivion.

My new buddy and I developed a great friendship, mostly built on finding and procuring drugs. One day, it occurred to me that this guy seemed to have a lot of money to spend, but it didn't seem like he had a reliable job or an obvious source of income.

"Hey man, can you find ecstasy?" he asked.

I was sure I could. By now, I had connections. "How many?"

I heard him say the number, but I wondered if I had heard it wrong. "One *hundred?*" I repeated.

Over the following months, a pattern was established. *Drug dealer* was a term I refused to actually think about. I was just doing what I had to do.

My buddy and I eventually decided I would need a third roommate to help with expenses. That decision opened a new chapter of my journey into the realm of drug use.

"Hey, can you get cocaine?" I asked my new roommate. I was already high. I just needed more. I needed to keep the high.

The new roommate grabbed his car keys. "I can be back in an hour. Give me $1,000."

My buddy and I looked at each other, shrugged, then left to go to the bank.

We used coke all night and all the next day. Then, we used it the next night. And the next. Days turned into weeks. Weeks turned into months. From starting with just a few grams, we graduated to using ounces every night. There were no lines between right and wrong. Stealing coke from my roommate was just a solution to a problem. My nose and gums were constantly bleeding, and my teeth were loose. So, snorting cocaine gave way to smoking crack. I couldn't stop. Addiction owned me. Euphoria beckoned. So what? Resistance was fruitless. In fact, resistance was never on my mind.

Before long, my friend announced that he was going back to his home up north. He had burned through all his money.

Now what would I do?

I had lost my job. I was penniless too. Every dime I had was used to support my habit. No one was paying the bills. The electricity and the water had been turned off. An eviction was surely in the works.

The hot, summer, air–conditioner–less days were brutal. The humid nights brought no more comfort. My stomach growled from hunger, but the thought of eating made me feel sicker. I continued to smoke crack in the dark by the flickering light of a single candle. Sweat poured off the end of my nose, threatening to extinguish the flame from my lighter. With no water to flush, the stench from the bathroom permeated the whole space even through the closed door. I had tried to siphon water from my waterbed through a stolen hose, but it proved ineffective. Reality was elusive. I kept peering out through a slit in the blinds to see if the police were outside.

No one's there.

Take another hit.

Even the drugs couldn't smother the facts this time. I was a failure. I was an addict. The pain would never really stop. It was just a few months before my nineteenth birthday. Could I call my dad? Could I go home? Would home welcome me? Clouds rolled into my heart. The little boy who had left his dad and his home with such bravado cried out from the depths of the fierce storm brewing within my soul. I hated the reality that sliced me to my core.

I needed my dad.

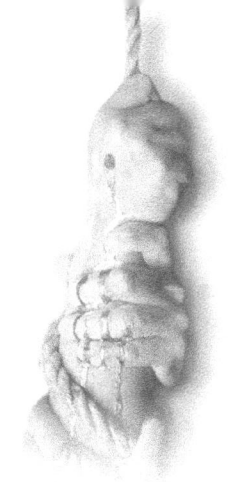

CHAPTER 7

EASY MONEY

Although it was an unfamiliar posture, I mustered up every bit of humility I could.

"Dad, can I come home?"

He consented, so I packed up my meager belongings and moved them into my dad's garage. Not long after moving back, I started a job delivering pizza, but I was still smoking crack every day. The cash tips were great, and I didn't have to pay rent. However, my habit was bigger than the tips and my paycheck so, when that was gone, I had to figure out how to get more money. I was desperate to continue supporting my habit, so I scoured the bags, boxes, and furniture in the garage for any dollar or coin that might have been dropped. Next, I started pawning everything that had any value at all . . . including the stereo—my pride and joy that I had worked all summer for. I sold jewelry and even gifts from family or friends. It was a terrible and painful solution, but at that moment, it was the only solution. I had to stay high. Anything I could get my hands on, I sold it. Before long, there was literally nothing left.

In fact, I pawned things so many times that my activity was flagged, and a detective came to my home. The police were pretty sure I had stolen the pawned items. My dad had to vouch for me that I was the rightful owner. They went away convinced, but I was sure they were planning to keep an eye on me.

Following my addict-logic, I guess my next line of thinking was inevitable. Remember, desperation has few boundaries. I was sure my dad had money in his room. One night when Cherie and Dad were out, I began a search for cash, which I didn't find. But I did find my mom's engagement ring. I knew she had left it to me, although I hadn't seen it in years. I could sell it. But something gripped me. Not even my desperation had power over this decision. I put it back.

I came across the PIN for a credit card in my dad's desk drawer.

"Jackpot!"

I seared the number in my brain and waited for my parents to go to sleep. The obsession was unyielding and took on a mind of its own. I was unable to control it. I had to get my hands on that card. That very night while they were sleeping, I snuck into Dad's room, found his wallet, and took the credit card. I slipped out the side door in the middle of the night and went straight to the bank.

The ATM was a drive-through. My nerves were on edge. I had to get the money. I punched in the number and waited while the machine hummed.

"Please take your cash" popped up on the screen.

Wow.

Endorphins kicked in. Excitement and anticipation consumed me. I drove immediately to the neighborhood where I knew I would find exactly what I needed. Within minutes, I scored and was filling my lungs with pure evil. Crack cocaine does not discriminate. It will steal the life of whoever samples it, crush it into an unrecognizable ball, and shatter it into a million pieces. I was instantly paranoid and numb at the same time. All the excruciating moments of brokenness and pain came to a head. I had crossed a line. Now, I had to keep going. I had no choice.

Back to the bank.

"Please take your cash."

More money. More crack. I tried withdrawing money a third time, but the bank wouldn't give me any more. It was 5:00 a.m. I had to go help a friend anyway. I hadn't had a real job for months, but I took any odd job offered to me for some quick cash.

I just needed a few dollars to keep going. I made it through a hot day of work. My phone vibrated in my pocket. It was my dad. Hesitation was pointless. I knew I had to answer.

"Michael, I had money stolen from my credit card last night. Before I call the police, was it you?"

The blood drained from my face, and I felt queasy. I tried to deny it, frantically trying to fabricate an explanation.

"Just be honest with me."

I was defeated. "Yeah, that was me. Don't worry. I'll move out. Just give me a few days."

I had nowhere to go. I drove back to my dad's house. I didn't need a few days. I would sneak in and pick up my stuff. But Dad was there, waiting for me. I handed him his card, packed my bag, and left. I had no idea what I was supposed to do, but I came up with a half-baked plan. I would find a parking area where I wouldn't be bothered. I would search for money during the day. At night, I could get high and barricade myself in my backseat.

Sensible decisions are not an addict's forte.

After spending several nights like this, I decided to make an attempt to join the Army. Not surprisingly, they didn't want me when I tested positive for drugs. After that, I found out my aunt was going up north to visit her mother, my grandmother. She asked if I would like to go. I said yes. It occurred to me that neither my dad nor my aunt had any clue what I was going through. They had no understanding of my slavery to this addiction. Maybe even I didn't really comprehend the severity of it.

This may be a great way to clear my head, I tried to reason as I muddled through the fog of the drugs.

Sitting at my grandmother's kitchen table, I was flooded with memories. I had been here with my mom and dad so many times before. Mom had eaten at this table.

"I was thinking about moving here to Vermont to spend time with you," I blurted out. This was not a plan I had previously made. I just knew I needed to get out of South Florida. Maybe a change in location was the solution.

A few weeks later, back in Florida, I was preparing to move to Vermont. I packed up everything I owned—which now fit into a couple of duffle bags. I just had some clothes and some shoes. My dad and I drove my barely sufficient 1986 Chevy Monte Carlo up to Grammy's house.

At first, it was okay to live at my grandmother's house. I had always loved Vermont. I was staying clean and helping my uncle on the farm. Eventually, I got a job at a lumber mill. After that, I moved from my grandmother's house into my own apartment. I started a relationship with a girl who lived next door. Soon, I began discovering I wouldn't survive without the drugs. I was craving cocaine or crack, but there was nothing available. I was asking the right people, though, and I soon learned I could easily get Oxycontin and heroin in abundance.

The job at the lumber mill was mostly outside. Vermont winters are hard, cold, depressing, and seem to last forever. I was a Florida boy, and I didn't think I would ever get warm again that winter. As the days and nights got colder, I became desperate. No matter what it took, I had to get high.

"Hey, man, can you get any pills?" If I hadn't gauged this co-worker correctly, my job was history.

"Yeah, I know someone."

Jackpot!

In less than an hour, I was in a bathroom snorting a crushed-up Oxycontin.

Relief.

Focus.

Okay, good. Now, how can I get more?

Like leeches attach to an unwary body, addiction's obsession will fasten itself to a soul with unbridled fury.

Huh, at least I'm free from the emotional turmoil.

The drugs lied to me. The immediate expectation of the results of using drugs is always consistent. The inevitable consequences of drug use are likewise.

In this case, the consequences soon became unavoidable. I lost my job, lost my girlfriend, lost all of my money, and lost my apartment. Besides all of that, I was beginning to detox and getting pretty sick. I called my dad again. It was decided I would go back to Florida and live with Dad and Cherie. Again.

Someone had offered me a job I could start right away, so I went back home to Dania Beach. But I wasn't safe. I wasn't free and I hadn't changed. My head was not cleared. The need for escape had only found another new address.

"You got a twenty?" I had found the dealer on the street corner. Having frequented this neighborhood in the past, every-one recognized me.

"Yeah, I got you."

I had only been back in Florida for a few hours, and I was already numb. Smoking crack kept the sickness at bay. In Vermont, I had seen a quack doctor who ran a pill mill. He kept me supplied with pain pills. I still had a bottle of Lortab.

Detoxing from opiates is excruciating to the body and the mind. Aches, pains, cravings, tremors, and vomiting are just a few symptoms. Paranoia, confusion, anxiety, and even delirium can overtake your mind and prevent normal thought patterns. I was determined to stay ahead of these symptoms by any means necessary.

My dad and Cherie would be home any minute. I knew Dad would come to my room to check on me. I had to come down from this high.

I took one Lortab. Nothing. I took another. No change. After several more, I passed out on my bed. Sharp pain startled me awake. I had to crawl to the bathroom. I was throwing up brown liquid. I counted. I had taken nine pills. Way too many.

Oh, God, I cried into the silence.

Please hear me.

Please help me.

I don't know how to stop.

CHAPTER 8

COPS AND CRACK COCAINE

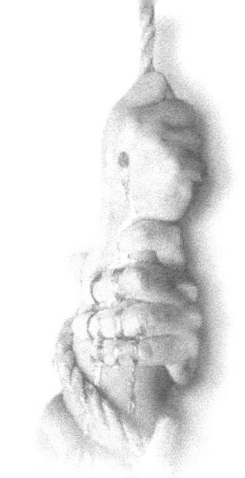

"Get out of the car."

This cop wasn't fooling around. Glancing in the rearview mirror, I saw the lights of at least three police cars behind me. Two more pulled up in front of me, blocking my car.

I rolled down the window but made no move to get out. "You have no probable cause to ask me to get out of my car." Rather audacious words from a guilty man who was higher than a kite.

"Oh, so you want to be a wise guy?" They surrounded the car. They opened the door and demanded I get out. "You are under arrest."

I had the good sense to be scared. I turned pale. They had me. Again. This was the second time in two weeks.

The first time, I had just left the neighborhood with a ten-dollar piece of crack. This place was notorious for drugs and gangs, so there was a fairly constant police presence. They had arrested me for Possession of Cocaine, and I spent the night in jail. Dad bailed me out the next day. Now, it would be another

$1,000 for another mess I had made. I was more than sure he would not bail me out again. I called anyway. *Hey, you never know.*

"Not this time." There was no hiding the disappointment in his voice.

The darkness of despair closed in as I sat on the concrete floor of the jail cell. I was having trouble taking regular breaths. Memories of Mom's disappointed face nagged at the edges of my mind. For the next few days, I felt like paralysis had set in. When I was finally able to talk to my dad again, I got some hopeful news.

"I contacted a friend, a criminal lawyer, who is willing to take your case." I wished Dad sounded as hopeful as I felt.

"Thank you, Dad." This was good, but it was going to get worse again. I had been writing bad checks and cashing them all over town. I would have to confess. But before I could, the post office confessed for me. My dad had received notices of thousands of dollars written in bad checks.

"Your father will have to pay off all the checks before charges are pressed for that also," the lawyer told me. Now with two felonies hanging over my head, the lawyer had to question how a judge might react.

I was in jail for twenty-two days. The detoxing had been ugly. I mostly stayed in a corner, away from the other inmates in general population. I doubt I had ever felt so totally alone, so totally abandoned. The pain was unyielding. I knew there was no hope for me to ever live a normal life like this. My thoughts went to God. But not for support. I wondered why He had created me just to be a worthless drug addict and a burden on my family.

"Cinelli!" My name was bellowed loudly and clearly into the recreation room.

I jumped up from the floor. Anxiety hit me in the pit of my stomach.

"Pack up your stuff. You're going home." The words meant nothing to the Corrections Officer. He was merely doing his job.

"What happened?"

The officer shrugged and kept moving.

It was bittersweet. I walked through the gates a free man. I was free from the jail cell, but still bound by the nothingness slowly demolishing my soul. Later, I learned the charges for the second felony, Possession of Cocaine, had been dropped. The lawyer, who was doing my dad a favor, proved the police had done an illegal search of my car which resulted in finding the coke. The first felony still stood. I would be facing a judge and the consequences of that.

I was out. So, where was I supposed to go? I called my dad. No answer. Then, I tried my uncle. Again, no answer. I remembered one other phone number. It happened to be my ex-girlfriend from my teenage years. *What the heck?* I dialed.

"Hello?"

I never believed she would really answer. "Um, hey, I just got out of jail. Any chance you could pick me up?"

"I'm on my way."

Whoa. What? We hadn't spoken in years. Not since the day we broke up.

Back at her house, she offered me a drink.

"I'll have a beer and a cigarette." Perhaps outwardly I was just a bit overconfident, but inside, I felt like screaming. I needed something, anything, to try to stop the gnawing pain.

The phone rang. She answered. Her face blanched. "Yeah, Mike is here."

She handed me the phone—it was my best friend. We had grown up together and had seen each other through a lot over the years.

Wait. Why was he calling her? We had all been childhood friends. I decided it was just a coincidence.

"Hey, man, I just got out of jail. We should hang out." A strange conversation starter for someone you hadn't seen or talked to in years.

"Yeah, that's a great idea."

A few days later, we did get together. I was confiding in my friend like old times. "I was hoping to get back on track and start dating my ex again," I told him. "It seems like maybe she still likes me."

He sort of agreed with me but didn't say much. That night, we went out to a party. When my friend's phone rang, I saw that it was from my ex-girlfriend. Finally, it became clear something was going on. So, I confronted him.

Yes, they were seeing each other.

"Yeah, man, we're going to get married."

The shock sent me reeling. The familiar pain of rejection cut deep.

So, nothing changes. Happy homecoming.

I asked my friend to take me home. The anger rose from deep in my chest. Those two were unbelievable.

Later, my friend called.

I hollered at the phone. "You listened to me tell you I wanted to date her again! You've been seeing each other all along! Why did you try to hide it?!" When he tried to respond, I cut him off. "I gotta go."

There was nothing left to do but get high. The dealer answered my call after two rings. Within an hour, I was curled up in the corner of my room, numb to the world. The hard white substance saved me. Every few minutes, it saved me again. And again. And again. The relief was so euphoric, but so short. I couldn't get enough.

Sixty days later, I was back in front of a judge. I was about to find out the consequences of my actions. I really hoped I wouldn't get more jail time.

"Drug Court." The lawyer made it sound like I had better agree.

"What is that?" I'm sure he heard the fear in my voice.

"It's a year-long program designed to prevent further drug use. It's very intense. There are lots of rules you will need to follow exactly. If you finish it, they will expunge your record."

Since I had been charged with Possession of Cocaine, this really was the only sensible option. I would do Drug Court.

I had to appear before a judge every thirty days and be drug tested twice a week. I relapsed numerous times. When the tests were positive for drugs, I was punished with more time in jail. I was sentenced to two more twenty-eight-day rehab programs, in addition to sixteen days at detox treatment centers. But after sixteen months of what I thought hell must feel like, I graduated from the Drug Court program. My record was expunged.

This time I'll stay clean.

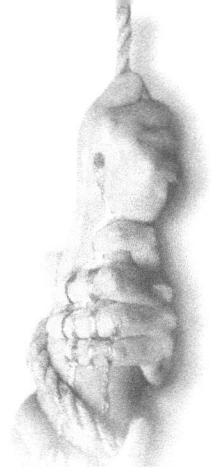

CHAPTER 9

HOMELESS AND HOT COFFEE

My record was erased. My addiction was alive and thriving.

I *wanted* to be clean. But I was in a twelve-foot rowboat with only one oar, trying to escape a forty-foot wave.

My dad had paid a lot of money to get me into another rehab. I had agreed to go, if only to sleep in a clean bed. Now, I wanted to get out of here, but I couldn't find a ride.

"I'll be there tomorrow around three o'clock." I had called a buddy I used to do drugs with. I'm sure he had good intentions.

That night, I lay in bed, overwhelmed with fear and pain. In desperation, I cried out, "Please help me, Lord?" I opened a book my aunt had given me, read a passage, and immediately felt peace enveloping me like a warm blanket on a chilly day.

God?

How many times had I heard my dad preach about His grace and His forgiveness? I felt empowered. I had to finish this journey.

The next day, my buddy never showed up. I didn't care. I knew what I needed to do. I completed the program. Then, I got into a halfway house. Then, I got a job. My family had been encouraging me for a long time to get help from counselors. I finally agreed and began talking to someone about my feelings. About my pain. At first, it felt kind of good. But my misery was too deep and the release of talking at therapy was too inconsistent. At least the pain caused by using drugs was less than the pain from dealing with my past.

Numbness was the only answer.

In a few short months, I had locked myself in the halfway house bathroom. Peeking out the window, I looked for the imaginary SWAT team hiding in the trees outside.

What am I doing?

Any minute someone could come in and catch me getting high. I didn't care. This was what I needed.

Boom, boom, boom!

Someone was banging on the bathroom door. There was nowhere to hide. The house manager caught me red-handed.

"What are you doing?"

The crack pipe in my left hand and the lighter in my right sufficiently answered his question.

Scared and defeated, I grabbed some clothes, threw them in a bag, and left the house. I was too high to think straight. Crack-induced paranoia gripped my brain. I had to lie down. My aunt's house wasn't too far. I snuck into her backyard and curled up in the dirt under an awning. I used an old towel I had shoved into the bag as a scanty blanket. Rain soaked my shoulder. I began to fall asleep. Fear and nightmares swirled around in my mind. Severe anxiety threatened my sanity. My veins throbbed from the poison I had ingested. I needed money. I needed to stay high. I needed to flee the pressure of the shame of what I had become. I got up and started walking again.

My phone hadn't died yet. An old drug-using buddy answered and was happy to help me out. An hour later, I was high again and we were headed to my buddy's apartment. We mixed cocaine in water and melted crack in vinegar so we could inject the drugs. My mission was to never stop being high.

Suddenly, my head dropped backward and my eyes went black.

"Are you okay?" My buddy was yelling frantically. He dumped a glass of water on my head. "Should I call an ambulance?"

I heard his shouts and began to come around. My eyes were blurry. "No, no, no. No ambulance." I barely got my mouth around those words.

I had loaded the needle with a big rock of cocaine. I knew it was going to be bad, but this was beyond my thinking. Many times, the idea of simply never waking up was comforting. But the reality of it scared the daylights out of me.

After that incident, my buddy started nit-picking and fault-finding. It was obviously time to move on. By now, my belongings fit into a backpack. I stuffed everything in there and headed out. I called another using buddy and asked if he had a place to stay.

"Nope, I'm sleeping in my dad's backyard. If you want, we can hang out and have each other's back."

"Okay, I'm on my way." I wasn't having rational thoughts. We had no money. Where on earth did we think we could stay?

We found the answer behind a strip mall. I spotted two mattresses behind a dumpster. They looked promising. They had been there awhile. The rusty springs were exposed. We pulled a few pieces of cardboard and Styrofoam from the dumpster. They provided less than ideal protection from the rain and hot sun, but they would do.

This was home for several weeks. Still, the voices wouldn't leave me alone.

You'll never amount to anything more than this. You belong here.

I couldn't allow my mind to clear from the drugs or the shame and the pain would finish me.

One morning, I woke up to find a small plate with two steaming cups of coffee and two warm donuts. Scanning the area, I saw no one. It was quiet. My tears of gratitude surprised me.

Again, I thought, *God? Could He really still care about me?* My buddy and I enjoyed our little breakfast and headed out.

We had been stealing merchandise and food from stores to sell for cash or to trade for drugs. One afternoon, several packages of stolen meat made a good trade for Xanax. We helped ourselves to one each and headed back to our "home." As we rounded the corner, we heard yelling, so we hid behind the wall to see what was happening. Two men were standing over our beds pouring something out of a gallon jug over everything we owned.

"What are those guys doing? That looks like vinegar."

We ran to survey the damage and see if anything was salvageable. Nope, everything was soaked in vinegar. The new acidic addition made sleeping there impossible.

Helping ourselves to another Xanax, we began walking with no destination in mind. We stole a cell phone from an open garage. The owner saw us, but we were faster than him. We got away and headed to a dealer's house to trade the phone for crack.

Suddenly, a truck skidded to a stop in front of us. It was the cell phone's owner. He rushed toward me, waving something in his fist.

Bang! I saw stars.

The large flashlight in the driver's hand had hit its target. Blood ran down my face. I guess the guy decided the phone wasn't worth getting into trouble for, because I still held it in my left hand and heard the truck driving away.

My friend and I made the deal. The phone for a ten-dollar rock. The blood on my face meant nothing to the dealer. Wasn't his problem.

At a nearby gas station, my buddy and I both used the bathroom, but not for nature calls. The crack did what crack does. It didn't last long. More Xanax would have to do. I stole a bottle of peroxide for the open wound on my forehead. We tried approaching some people for money, but that just got us kicked out. Continuing to wander the streets, I pulled a backpack out of an unlocked parked car. The Xanax was doing its thing. We had to rest on a curb.

Eventually, my buddy got up and made an announcement. "I'm going to my ex-girlfriend's house."

I reminded him I had nowhere to go. He just kept walking. I guess it was every man for himself. Way to have my back.

Alone and so tired, I sprawled out on the soft grass next to the curb. The Xanax had done its job. Sleep took over without a fight.

In the early morning hours, I woke up to silence. I was cold. I had no idea where I was or what had happened. My mind was flashing memories. *Sprinklers. Backpack. Putting clothing on.* I looked down at my body. I was wearing a clown costume. Colorful frilly sleeves and fluffy balls for buttons. Humiliation broke through the drug daze.

Looking up to the sky, I said out loud, "What am I doing?" Did God see me now? I needed to be rescued.

Somehow, I covered the several miles to my dad's house. It was do or die. The voices accompanied me all the way.

This is useless. They're done with you. You're nothing but a worthless addict.

I was a little surprised that anyone heard my timid knock. Looking my dad in the face would require more courage than I could rally. I spoke to the floor. "I need help."

The door opened wide. I accepted the invitation.

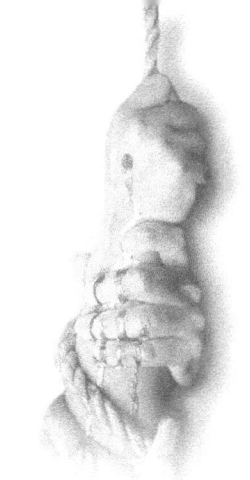

CHAPTER 10

GO BIG OR GO HOME

"Mike, are you okay?" I think my dad was trying to keep one eye on the road and one on me.

"Nah, I'm feeling tired. And pretty sick." I was beginning to detox from the opiates I had been using. My profusely running nose and teary eyes made it look like I was crying. My stomach was in knots. I tried hard to control the nausea. I didn't want to throw up in the car.

We were on the way to Fort Myers. I was entering a rehab program at a place called Teen Challenge—a one-year residential program. I had no idea what to expect. Apprehension crept up my spine. A whole year! Up to then, I hadn't been clean for more than a month.

My skin was crawling from the withdrawal symptoms. My body wanted to run. I knew how to make the pain stop. My mind raced as I imagined a list of reasons I might use to get my dad to turn around and take me home. I could live with them. I had promised myself I would stay clean this time.

The truth nagged at me. *Who am I kidding? I can't stay clean on my own.*

We arrived at our destination. I decided I would dig in and give it a try. Dad was pretty upset about all the relapses. Today, he was happy he wouldn't have to wonder where I was and if I was safe. We said our goodbyes and he was gone.

The place looked normal. Everyone had a bed, and I got to choose the top bunk or bottom. Eight guys used only one bathroom, so that was rough. That first night, I couldn't sleep at all. I was feeling really sick, and the guy on the bottom bunk got up to use the bathroom an awful lot. I counted six times. No doubt he was using coke. I wanted some so much that it hurt. All the pain from the last twenty years pressed my chest, as anxiety crushed my lungs. I could hardly breathe. Rebellion came to my rescue. The next day, I would make it my goal to find out how to get high.

"You want to eat breakfast?"

"No," I managed a muffled grunt. Pain ruled. Physical. Emotional. I would just stay in bed. I spent the rest of the day in and out of consciousness.

"Do you want something to eat?"

Another grunt.

I was beginning to obsess about getting drugs. Eventually, I snuck out and went down the street to a corner market. I bought cigarettes and, just for fun, Skittles. Addicts love the tiny sugar high. Behind the building, I smoked one. I was so nervous; I nearly burned my hand with the match. I needed to find the guy sleeping on the bottom bunk.

"I have to get out of here," I mumbled. A staff member walked by. "Who do I talk to if I want to leave?"

"You would have to talk to the Program Director."

I thanked him as he led me to the director's office. As I sat down, I noticed the outline of the cigarette box in my pocket. I hoped he didn't. I began to feel very nervous.

"I want to leave." I was doing my best "I mean it" impression.

The director was kind. He smiled. "Why would you want to do that?"

I didn't want to look at him. He was right. I had nowhere to go.

Teen Challenge is a Christian organization. They employ a biblical resolution to recovery. Every client knows that going in. The director began to recount his own life story. He had been on a destructive path. He told me how an encounter with Jesus Christ had changed and redirected him. He discovered that there really was a way to live a better life.

He stopped. "Is there anything you need to tell me?"

Yeah, he saw the cigarettes. My face revealed my guilt. "I have these," I blurted out. I grabbed the cigarette box and matches and handed them over. I kept the Skittles.

That one good decision was a defining moment. A peace I was sure only God could provide enveloped me. I left the director and went back to my room. When Bottom-Bunk-Guy walked in, I wanted to ask him about his many trips to the bathroom last night, but I didn't. From somewhere, in the deepest part of me, a flicker of hope arose. I made the choice to keep doing the right thing. I wanted to know if there actually was a better life ahead. I truly meant it.

In the morning, I felt a little better, although I hadn't slept for a few days. I was tired and couldn't eat, so I headed toward my room after breakfast to lie down. It seemed unusually quiet, and I wondered where everyone had gone. In my room, six out of the eight people staying there were packing their bags.

A staff member leaned against the door watching them.

"Where's everyone going?"

"They are all leaving. That's all I can say for now."

Later, a meeting was called. The director stood up and explained what had happened. One of the guys had purchased drugs from someone who lived on the same street where Teen Challenge was located. He had passed them out to nine other guys. "I've asked them all to pack their things and leave."

I couldn't believe what I was hearing. That could have been me. I decided right then that I would stick it out. I would do whatever I had to do. Determination became my middle name.

The next day, the director was assigning job responsibilities. Although I couldn't list any useful skills, I did know I could work hard and learn fast.

"Mike, you're in the kitchen."

Okay. I always enjoyed cooking. If the Army had wanted me, I would have been a cook. Their loss. I was excited. Apprehensive. I decided that I would do this program like I did drugs. *If you're going to do it, do it well. Go big or go home, right?*

I put everything I had into that program. They told me to read the Bible every day. I did. They told me to write in a journal and create a list of people to pray for. I did. They told me to wash dishes and to scrub the toilets and floors. I did. I noticed something beginning to happen in my heart. I felt content. I began to think about who I was and who I wanted to become. I didn't like what I was seeing. I finally admitted I was filled with so much anger. Anger at a God Who would let my mom die. Anger at my mom for abandoning me when I needed her. Anger at my dad for replacing my mom with someone else and deserting me when I needed him most. Anger at my stepmother for coming between me and my dad.

What was going to happen to me? What about my future?

I had no skills, no degrees, no money, and bad credit. I had a criminal record. No woman in her right mind would ever want to be with me. Yet, I could not deny the hope that was growing in the very depths of my soul. I dared to believe that God had given me life for a purpose. I resolved to keep looking for it.

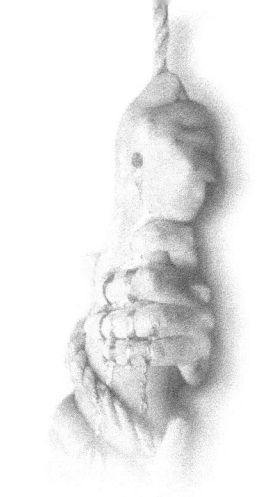

CHAPTER 11

STARTING OVER

After twelve months, I completed the rehab program. I was a changed man. When I graduated, Teen Challenge put me to work for them as the kitchen manager. I worked for room and board. Free food and a warm bed were good enough payment for me right now. I had nowhere else to go—addiction was exhausting. After just four months, they gave me the opportunity to develop an auto detailing business for the program. Through my different positions, I gained leadership and business skills, and learned how to handle people. These were life skills God knew I needed to acquire. My abilities were recognized. Within five months, I was promoted to program director.

As good as all this was, I still carried in my heart a strong desire to go to school. At the age of twenty-seven, I applied and was accepted to a leadership training program in Jacksonville, Florida. But, before the start of classes, I learned that the program had been discontinued. What a disappointment. I had to call the school to request the return of my deposit.

The nice lady who took my call asked me, "Have you heard about the Teen Challenge in Pennsylvania? They've received an offer from an accredited college to provide classes to graduates from the Teen Challenge program."

I called Pennsylvania right away. Another sweet lady answered the phone. "That's right!" She might never know just how much her cheerful voice encouraged me. "We offer classes for college credits. You only need a high school diploma or a GED and proof of your graduation from Teen Challenge."

I could provide those items. I had been homeschooled, so I did not have a diploma from a high school. Thank God my aunt had basically forced me to get my GED. I remember that encounter vividly.

"We have an appointment to get your GED. I'm picking you up tomorrow morning whether you are ready or not." My Aunt Kathy told me this in her "don't argue with me" tone.

I didn't feel ready, but I knew I didn't have a choice. Fear had convinced me I could never pass the test. That, and the fact that I hadn't attended any of the classes. If (or when) I failed, it would just prove how stupid I truly was.

I had to get high to navigate these emotions. I went back to the neighborhood, walking up and down each street looking for "the nod." Ah, there he is.

"Can I get a twenty?"

Back at my apartment, I smoked until it was all gone. In a paranoid stupor, I looked out through the blinds. There was no one outside, but the voices hovered inside my head.

You're still a loser. You will never amount to anything useful.

Cowering in my bed, I tried to figure out what to do. My mind raced. I was sure I'd never sleep that night.

A loud knocking on my door woke me up. My aunt meant business. Shaking and blurry-eyed, I let her in.

"Get ready," she said. I hadn't expected her to really show up. I searched hard for a good excuse. Nope. No chance of getting out of it.

She dropped me off to take the test and gave me ten dollars for lunch. I was there and had nothing else to do, so I took the test. From somewhere in my gut, I felt like the wisest plan was to just give it my best effort. And I did. When the results came back a couple of weeks later, I was thrilled. I had passed! I had my GED. My eyes filled with tears as I recalled my aunt's belief in me and our conversation.

"I never thought I was very smart," I had told her.

"Miggy," she said, using the nickname she had given me, "you can do anything you put your mind to."

I submitted the application to the school in Pennsylvania, fully expecting to be rejected. But the opposite happened—I was accepted! Dad and I packed up my little Chevy Cavalier and set off on the long drive to Rehrersburg, PA. I was nervous and apprehensive, so during the hours on the road, I prayed. I asked God to give me the strength and wisdom I would need to succeed. As I was praying, I watched my dad. One fact hit me hard.

My dad always shows up.

Memories of his showing up caused my chest to tighten with emotion . . . three years ago, he had shown up just like he was now.

I was waiting for my dad to pick me up to take me to a detox facility. I had used up my last option. I had been living in my car. Hadn't slept for days. The syringe filled with brown liquid would be the last injection before the miserable detoxing took over my mind and body. The warmth spread through my shoulders and up the back of my neck. Seconds later, I was numb.

At the facility, I managed to get to the front desk and put my name on the list. "We will call you when we have a bed ready."

It was early, so it was still dark outside. I saw Dad sitting on a bench, waiting for me. I barely made it to him before collapsing.

Dad held me and gently placed my head on his shoulder. I tried to open my eyes, but I couldn't see clearly. My feet were wet. It was raining. I felt myself drooling. I couldn't raise my head. Dad didn't move. We waited in the rain for hours. Dad continued to hold me tight, his shoulder soaked with my saliva. Not talking, just making sure I was still breathing.

After some time, I was able to muster up some courage to mumble, "I'm sorry, Dad."

"I'm here. I'm not going anywhere. Stay with me. We lost your mom. I can't lose you too."

"I won't ever leave you again," I whispered to myself. *I sincerely hoped this wish would come true.*

As I continued to watch Dad in the car, I realized what a meaningful trip this was for him and me. We hadn't been able to connect with one another for years. I was finally clean and thinking clearly. We were having significant conversations. Despite the ever-present sorrow and grief, an inkling of hope seeped into my heart.

We made it to our destination. I dropped Dad off at the airport and reported to the school to begin my new life. I moved into the apartment that they provided, and met my roommate who would soon become one of my best friends. I loved this school and all the classes. I was doing well. My GPA was 3.75. I made other great friends at the school and at the church I started attending. I began to feel content again. Purpose had finally begun to infiltrate my thinking. I was working hard to rekindle the relationship I once had with God in my youth.

Pennsylvania, unlike Florida, has definite season changes. By November, the balmy days of summer were turning into the crisp days of fall. I seriously dislike cold weather. As the falling leaves turned from orange to brown and a constant chill permeated the air, my contentment gave way to restlessness, loneliness, and even desperation. I wanted to feel loved. I had recently contacted an old girlfriend from Florida, and I found comfort in confiding in her. I wanted to believe that God had future plans for me. I began to hope that this girl would be included, and I became impatient with the waiting. I could move faster on my own.

A few months later, I called the director from the Teen Challenge in Florida. We had a long conversation and caught up. As we said our goodbyes, he spoke some polite parting words I couldn't ignore: "We sure would like to have you back someday."

"Really!?" I was beyond excited. I hadn't expected to hear that. I wasn't about to let this idea go. My mind raced. Familiarity sounded so comforting. And it would bring me close to that old girlfriend.

What a good idea to move back. I talked to my dad and others for counsel. Well, I told them part of the whole story. I didn't want to let them know that I suspected it wasn't a good idea. I just wanted to make this happen, no matter what. The Teen Challenge director officially offered me a job. In a few short weeks, I was all set. I had a place to live, a job, and a potential girlfriend. What more could I need?

Only it wasn't exactly all set.

"I don't think this is actually going to work out," my ex–girlfriend said as I told her my plans. Her words pierced my heart and soul with a rejection I couldn't bear. She had seen my insecurities, my neediness. She was not impressed. "You called me fifteen times in a row!"

My excuse that I thought her phone was turned off didn't cut it. We said our goodbyes. The pain was deep. The disappointment was deeper. I lay awake in my bed trying to figure out how to fix this. The lies were louder than the reasoning.

You are right. You are worthless. You will never be good enough. You are destined to be a failure. If there was an enemy of my soul, he was on the prowl and he was relentless.

Then, I heard another voice. *Don't go!*

My heart sank. My stomach turned. I couldn't prove it, but I was quite sure it was God speaking. Hadn't I asked Him to speak to me?

But it's too late to back out now. I was groaning, maybe whining, in response. Everything was packed. It was all set. How could I turn back on my plans?

"I've been clean for three years," I said out loud. "I will be just fine." It was a valiant thought mixed with a dollop of bravado.

Somehow that reassurance sounded like no reassurance at all.

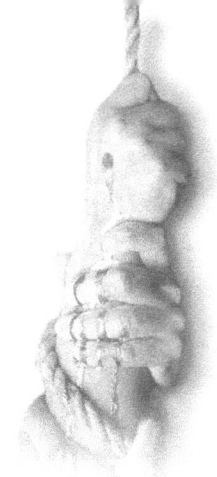

CHAPTER 12

CHICKEN WINGS AND GUEST ROOMS

It took a few months for me to get re-settled at the Teen Challenge in Fort Myers. It took even less time to realize that I didn't much enjoy the job they had given me. Loneliness came creeping back into my heart. I wasn't sure what "normal" should feel like, but I wanted to experience going out and doing what I thought "normal" people did. It started with a speed dating get-together the local radio station was doing. I mean, it was a Christian radio station, for goodness' sake! It must be okay.

After the get-together, I started going out on dates. I kept looking for someone who could dispel this loneliness.

One day, I had buffalo wings on my mind. A couple of the guys agreed to join me at the local sports bar. The server was extra attentive as she seated us. It sure seemed like she was flirting. But my unhealthy self-esteem imagined I was making it up.

No, that was definitely a flirty smile. She placed the receipt on the table.

"Bet you won't leave your number on the receipt," my friend said to me jokingly. His comment proved he had noticed it as well. So, it wasn't in my head . . .

"Bet I will," I said boldly. The tiniest sense of guilt warned me I was flirting too—flirting with fire. I paid the bill and started to leave. But then I had a second thought. I ran back to the table and wrote my number on the receipt.

We joked about it on the way home. I was pretty confident that I'd never hear from her.

Ding! A text popped up on my phone. I had only been home for a couple of hours.

"Hey, do you remember me?"

I didn't recognize the number. *"Who is this?"*

"You left your number on the receipt at my restaurant."

Wow! She actually responded to me. We began to text each other every day. We talked on the phone every night before bed. My longing for companionship was overpowering my sense of caution.

"Can I see you?"

"Sure, I get off at five o'clock. Do you want to come over to my house?"

I was headed for the cliff. *"Yes."*

I knew what would happen if I followed this path. The war in my soul was genuine. I had become serious about living a life that would honor God. But I was a little more serious about filling the void caused by my loneliness. Trying to trick God by continuing to struggle was obvious to both of us. Couldn't He see I needed this? I straightened my back and told reason to take a hike. Fear of losing what I might have with her drove me onward. I would spend the night with her.

Early the next morning, I jumped up in panic and maybe a tiny dash of remorse. I was living in one of Teen Challenge's graduate houses with a group of other guys, and I needed to get back home before anyone became suspicious. The morning shift workers would see that I wasn't home.

So, this is what it feels like to be double-minded. I hoped God had His eye on some other sinner. The guilt was rather unpleasant. I would have to tell someone.

Confession was not one of my better skills, but the pastor's office felt safe. "Can I tell you something?" I decided to ease into my confession. "I've been seeing someone. We are getting serious."

"Have you slept with her?" The pastor was jumping right in.

"Umm, yes. That's why I'm here. I want to do this the right way. We'll stop. Maybe you could counsel us." This wasn't going as I had hoped.

"I'll have to speak to the director. We'll get back to you."

I left his office dejected and distraught. My own self-loathing self-talk had already convinced me that I was worthless and undeserving of the pastor's consideration. I had no idea what to expect.

I received a phone call and was summoned to the director's office. I sat down to hear whatever he had to say.

"I'm sorry, Mike. We're going to have to let you go. You have a week to move all of your things out." The director's words echoed off the thick walls of grief and pain my past had erected around my heart.

Rejected again. *How could I have imagined this* wouldn't *happen?* I briefly wondered how many times he had had to say those words. *Did he like this part of the job?*

Tears waited behind my eyes as I packed my meager belongings. Where was I going to go? A new kind of fear loitered in my gut. I had begun to renew a relationship with a God I had long forgotten. I had dared to believe again. But I was a disappointment. Would He give up on me now, as well?

"You can come stay here if you want," my new girlfriend told me. We had only known each other for two weeks. I promised her, and myself, it would be temporary. Secretly, I was excited to be with someone who apparently cared about me. I was curious to see where this would go.

It only took a few days to find out. She became distant and seemingly uninterested. She was pushing me away. Anger felt like the best response to another rejection.

"I got fired from my job for you. I gave up everything I have been working for." Blaming her released me from having to take responsibility for my own decisions. Yelling at her further convinced me it was her fault.

I was able to find a job, so I began to look for a place to rent. I answered an ad for a room to rent in someone's apartment. I would be living in their guest bedroom. No problem. I was used to living with strangers. They agreed to split the deposit over two weeks. Now to get my things and tell my "girlfriend" that I was moving out.

She wasn't home. I packed, set the key on the end table, and closed the door. She pulled in as I was headed for my car.

My nervousness surprised me. "I packed all my stuff. I've rented my own place."

Nothing. No response. She ignored me as if I wasn't there. She walked into the house without as much as a glance. I was crushed. My heart heaved in my chest. I would have preferred a fight. Any interaction might have raised my worth to a little more than zero.

I wonder if I can get heroin around here.

No, no, no, no. You've been clean and sober for more than three years.

The voice of misery was louder. If I was going to be miserable, I might as well be high. The pre-relapse war raged in my heart and in my soul. Completely lost. Completely alone. *How could I have let myself get back here?* I was too tired to fight. For now, I was even too tired to give in.

I'm not sure why I even spoke to this girl again, but we started talking for a couple more weeks. It seemed like we might be able to work things out and get back together.

"Maybe we can rent an apartment together," she told me.

Whoa! Okay, maybe we could. It would force us to work together. I wouldn't be lonely anymore.

"Sign here and right here." I was signing the lease. Reason tried to emerge from the fog of emotional turmoil. I waved it off.

"I'll start bringing my things over in the morning," I told her.

"Oh, wait, you're not moving in with me."

What???

"I just rented an apartment in my name and you're telling me I can't live there?" I was fuming. I had let myself become vulnerable. She used me. She scammed me.

Back in my room, I nestled into the pain. We were good friends by now. I could count on the misery. It remained faithful. My dad always preached that God was faithful.

Maybe He would help me. Maybe He would heal me.

Nah. He didn't stop my mom from dying. She was a good person. Why would He think of me—a drug-addicted loser?

I knew what would take away this torment . . .

I saw the head nod as I drove by. The guy was on foot. We made eye contact and the dealer ducked into an alley. I was looking for heroin, but at this point, anything would do. I spun the wheel and U-turned into the alley.

"You got that boy?" I have to admit I was a bit apprehensive having not done this for three years.

"Nah, I got that girl, though." The guy held out four small yellowish chunks of pure relief for me to see. My heart skipped a beat with excitement. My stomach churned in anticipation. Better judgment had fled when I turned down this street.

"Let me get a forty." I grabbed two twenty-dollar crack rocks. Minutes later, I was exhaling a thick cloud of white solace. This was so good. And so bad. Within seconds, the paranoia overpowered me.

Someone will find out. The cops are behind me. I don't have any more money.

I need another hit.

The thoughts were menacing, crushing. But they served me well. They drowned out my other thoughts about failure and shame.

My fingertips were black from the soot left behind by the lighter. They ached from holding the crack pipe so tight I was almost unable to let it go. The paranoia held me in a frozen state.

This will be my last hit.

No. I have to get more. I have to get more, no matter what.

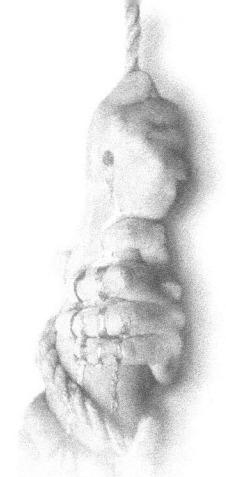

CHAPTER 13

PAWN SHOPS AND HANDCUFFS

"We're going camping," my landlords told me. They would be out of the house all weekend. I would finally be alone. I nonchalantly waved them goodbye. They locked their bedroom door and were off. I had been getting high for several days and I knew I wouldn't stop.

The dealer answered his phone right away. "Let me get a hundo."

I drove into the parking lot of the fast-food restaurant where we agreed to meet. I stared at the five twenty-dollar crack rocks the dealer dropped in my hand. I couldn't get back to my room fast enough. Anticipation roiled in my gut. I had to get the next hit.

Ahhh.

The lighter, the sizzle, the smoke. Sadly, the paranoia was part of the package.

What if they come home early?

Maybe they would, but I couldn't quit. I was on a mission to numb any emotion, and I soon lost the ability to care.

I had already been back to the dealer four more times. The obsession would not stop. I was out again, and I needed to get more. My next actions were inevitable. A kitchen knife and very little effort opened the locked bedroom door. Any kind of jewelry would do. I left the gold necklace and ring on the nightstand. *Too obvious.* I found a gold ring in a drawer. *Jackpot.*

The pawn shop gave me $200. I went straight back to the dealer, then straight back to my room.

I can't stop. I can't stop.

Was I making a confession or a plea for help? It didn't matter. In a few hours, I was out again. I only had one option left. The absence of the gold necklace and ring made the nightstand obviously empty.

I'll deal with the consequences later.

It was the same story once again. Pawn shop. Dealer. My room. Out again in a few hours.

My desperation was beginning to scare me. I was about to commit another serious crime. I had the keys to the place where I worked. Just recently, I was given the code to open the safe. It was 1:30 a.m. My nerves were on high alert. I had to unlock the front doors, get into the safe, and grab the money before the security guards drove by.

Just twenty dollars, I decided. Hands shaking, I opened the money bag. *Okay, just forty dollars.* I stuffed the two twenties into my pocket. Despite my shaking, I managed to lock the safe and leave everything as I found it.

I made it.

I sighed in relief as I jumped into my car. Back to the dealer. Two twenty-dollar rocks. Back to my room to smoke.

"That went far too fast," I spoke out loud to the empty room. It was 4:30 a.m. I didn't care. It was a quick trip back to my workplace. This time, I didn't give myself a limit. I would simply take all the cash in the money bag. For a moment, the weight of the shame almost stopped me. But the need was too great. I grabbed the stack of money, locked the safe and the front door, and dashed to my car.

"Hey, what are you doing here at this time?" The voice from behind stopped me in my tracks.

The flashing yellow lights almost blinded me. My paranoia made me question if this was real. I hadn't slept in about five days. My sense of reality was faulty. I turned and saw the security guard leaning out of his car. Whatever answer I gave had to be good.

"We're doing inventory this morning. My boss isn't here yet. I was going to go grab some breakfast and come back." Believable. Surely this guy had already called the police. I listened for the sirens. In truth, there was a little spark of relief that I had been caught. I knew I would never stop until something stopped me.

"Okay, just make sure you let the office know next time."

Man, I was getting good at this. Some security guy he was.

I nodded my head and jumped in my car, shaken to my core with fear. Even that encounter still wasn't enough to stop me. Deep down, I hated thinking of the aftermath of all this.

I don't have to deal with that today.

Very soon, those thoughts and emotions would be annihilated anyway. The money in the bag ended up not being much, but it was enough to buy me a journey to a place that would feel like home. I watched the dealer count my money as I drove away. When I got to the house, I locked myself in my room and picked up my lighter.

I heard noises. It sounded like people were going in and out of the apartment. I must have fallen asleep. There was talking outside of my bedroom door.

"We'll let you know what we find." The "10-4" response from the radio confirmed they were cops.

Fear wrapped its tentacles around my throat. I gulped for breath. I was stuck. I threw whatever personal items I could find in the dark into a suitcase and waited. I needed to get out. What if they were just waiting in the living room to catch me?

Hours went by. I sat immobilized by terror. Then, I heard more noises. Someone was leaving the apartment. I cracked the bedroom door. I could see the back of somebody's head through the balcony doors. His back was to me and the sliding glass doors were closed. I had half a chance to make it out.

Grabbing the suitcase, I slipped out the bedroom door. Just like in the movies, I clung to the wall and ducked to almost a crawl. The six-foot-long hallway seemed like a mile to the front door. The handle turned quietly, and the door swung open without a sound. I ran like a bear was chasing me and jumped in my car. Adrenaline shot blood to my muscles, causing my arms and legs to tremble wildly. My blood pressure must have gone sky-high. Driving wasn't going to be easy, but I had to get away.

Eventually, my breathing slowed and my body calmed down. I checked the rearview mirror. No cops.

Now what?

There was only one person to call. I grabbed my phone.

"Hey, Dad, can I come visit you guys?" Casual. Convincing. I couldn't let on that I was in any trouble.

"Sure."

"I'm on my way." It would be a two-and-a-half-hour drive across Alligator Alley to Fort Lauderdale. That's a long enough time to be alone while shame and failure pummel you mercilessly. Oh, yeah, I was in a big mess. The constant hum of the pavement and the *zing zing* of the passing cars soothed me into a dubious sense of peace.

Ding. A text.

Ding. I saw the name on the screen. It was the woman whose jewelry I had stolen.

Ding. Three texts. They must have figured it out. It took all my courage to read the messages.

"We know it was you. The police took fingerprints. Why did you steal my jewelry?" I liked this person. In another life, I might have been friends with her. Panic set in. If I ignored this, maybe it would all go away.

Ding.

Okay, I couldn't ignore it.

"If I'm able to recover all your jewelry, will you drop any charges and let me get my belongings back?" Except for what was in the small suitcase, I had left everything I owned in my room.

She agreed. What I knew I had to do next terrified me.

"Uh, Dad, can I talk to you for a second?" I was getting way too much practice at confession. "I stole jewelry from the people I was renting a room from. I pawned it for cash so I could get high. The police know it was me. If I can get it back to the owner, she'll drop the charges."

"How much?" My heart broke again at his sigh of realization and disappointment.

I really want to stop using drugs. I really do.

"Here's the money you need. Go get this lady's jewelry back and come straight home."

I couldn't meet his eyes. I had to force myself to get back into my car. Two and a half more hours of excruciating pain. This time, the hum of the pavement screamed words of condemnation mile after mile.

Stupid. Loser. Failure. Addict. I wished I could just disappear somehow.

"I need to buy back the jewelry I pawned a couple of days ago."

The pawn shop owner eyed me suspiciously. "Why?"

"Well, I just decided I want to keep it." I hoped there would be no more questions.

The guy disappeared behind a door. In a few minutes, he came back with the jewelry. *This may actually work.* I paid him and walked out.

One more to go. The second pawn shop let me buy back the jewelry without question. I texted the owner of the stolen goods.

"I have all your jewelry."

"Come drop it off and you can get your things."

Anxiety and regret accompanied me back to her house. I handed her the plastic bag which she dumped out to examine the contents. She was angry. But she still regarded me with some compassion. "Pack your stuff."

I loaded my car, got on the highway, and headed back across the state for the third time. My phone vibrated. I didn't recognize the number, but I answered anyway.

"Hello, I'm a detective with the Fort Myers police department. I was hoping you could come in and answer a few questions for me."

"Oh, well, I am on the road back to the East Coast. I can come in next week sometime." Yikes. Which crime caused this phone call?

"I really need you to come today." The detective was not taking no for an answer.

The lump of fear in my throat threatened to choke me. "Okay, I think I can make it there in twenty minutes." This was not good. My dad was going to find out everything.

The Fort Myers Police Department sign was not a welcome one. I was sure the woman behind the glass knew everything bad about me. I asked to see the detective, but I wasn't sure the desk clerk could hear me over the screaming voices in my head.

The detective came out from locked doors. "Come with me."

In his office, we both sat down. The fear cleared my mind of any rational thought. He spoke first. "Tell me your side of what happened on the night of October 28."

Try as I might, the best I could do was tell the truth. I gave him the facts as I remembered them.

"Give me a minute." The detective exited the room, leaving me alone for what seemed like an eternity.

When he came back, I took one look at him and I knew I wasn't going home. "I'm placing you under arrest. I will allow you to call your dad."

So, he wasn't entirely unfeeling.

I dialed the number. *Oh boy. How would I say this?* Again, the truth was the best idea. "Hey, Dad, I'm under arrest. I'll be going to county jail. My car is still here at the station."

I knew whatever words of rebuke Dad might have said right then wouldn't make any difference. I guess he knew it too. He only said, "Okay, son, I will come get your car."

I hung up just as another officer came into the room. "Get up and put your hands behind your back."

Cold steel clicked tightly around my wrists. If any dignity remained, it disappeared with that sound. They led me down the hall and left me alone in a ten-by-ten cell. This would be my third time in jail before I reached my thirtieth birthday. They didn't say it, but I could almost hear the words, "Now spend some time thinking about what you did."

Huh, as if that wasn't exactly what I would be doing.

11/06/2009 Filed Lee County Clerk of Courts-Criminal Division

OBTS No	Agency Report Number	**PROBABLE CAUSE STATEMENT**	1. Arrest (cont) 2. Notice to Appear (cont)	3. Arrest Affidavit 4. Complaint Affidavit 5. Request for Capias
Agency ORI Number FL████	Agency Arrest Number	Lee County Sheriff's Office	JUVENILE	

Defendant Name (last, first, middle)	Alias
Cinelli, Michael Angelo	

The undersigned certifies and swears that he/she has just and reasonable grounds to believe that the above named Defendant committed the following violation of law: STOLEN PROP-DEAL IN DEALING/TRAFFICKING IN STOLEN PROPERTY, LARC THEFT IS 300 OR MORE BUT LESS THAN 5000 DOLS
On the **29** day of **October** **2009** at **2142** ( ) A.M. (X) P.M. (Specifically include facts constituting cause for arrest.)

WRITE NARRATIVE IN THE 1st PERSON (i.e. I witnessed the suspect)   GIVE BASIS FOR KNOWLEDGE OF THE INCIDENT (i.e. I was told by)

Narrative

On Thursday, October 29, 2009 at approximately 2142 hours, while on uniform patrol in Lee County, Florida, Deputy ████ responded to ████ in reference to a past occurred theft of jewelry.

Deputy ████ made contact with the complainant and victim, ████████ a white female born on ████████ stated that on this date she and her husband noticed there were several pieces of jewelry missing from within their bedroom. According to ████ her husband placed his jewelry on his night stand on Tuesday night around 2000 hours. This morning around 0900 hours, he noticed his jewelry was gone. When ████ came home this evening she looked in her clothes drawers and realized some of her jewelry was missing as well.

████████ reports their roommate, Michael Angelo Cinelli, a white male born on July 09, 1981, may be responsible for stealing the jewelry. According to ████ she met Michael through an ad she placed on Craig's List while looking for a roommate. Michael Angelo Cinelli has been living in her home for approximately three weeks. She said that since he has moved in she and her husband try to keep their bedroom door locked when they are not home, however when they left the residence on Tuesday night they forgot. She believes that Michael Angelo Cinelli may be involved in drugs and may have stolen their jewelry for money or for drugs. ████ ensured Deputy ████ that no one else has access to the home other than herself, her husband, and Michael Angelo Cinelli.

Items missing from the home include a pair of 14k gold cross earrings, a woman's gold necklace with a heart pendant that has diamonds and "Mom" written in the middle, a man's wedding band, gold with diamonds and ████████ engraved inside, a men's gold link necklace with a solid gold cross charm, a men's gold link bracelet, and a woman's gold ring with an black onyx surrounded by diamonds. All items totaled in an estimated value of $2180.00.

Detective ████████ was assigned as the case detective. Detective ████ met with the ████████ at their residence. A detailed list of property that was stolen was taken by Detective ████ ████ states she confronted Michael Angelo Cinelli the day following the report. Michael Angelo Cinelli became upset and left the residence and all of his belongings with.

Since Michael Angelo Cinelli left he has text messaged her on numerous occasions indicating he wanted to get her property back to her. He stated he would buy it back and just wanted to keep law enforcement out of the picture.

The investigation identified the business of ████████ as a location where part of the property was sold. Detective ████ responded to this location and met with ████████ the Managing Director. ████ produced property that had recently been sold to them by Michael Angelo Cinelli. A men's wedding ring was turned over to Detective ████ Upon inspection the ring had the same engravings that were originally reported by ████ at the time of the report. A hold was placed on this property pending identification by this victim.

Detective ████ learned a business identified as ████████ located at ████████ was another popular location Michael Angelo Cinelli sold property to. Detective ████ met with the owner who states Michael Angelo Cinelli had been in earlier and purchased some property back from them that he had originally sold. The property described was consistent with property reported stolen.
(Continued)

Anuls Only		Date		
( ) Hold for First Appearance Do Not Bond Out. Reason:	B O N D			
I swear/affirm the above and reverse and attached statements are true and correct. OFFICERS SIGNATURE ████	D	Location of Appearance (Court Room No. Address)		
NAME (printed) **Detective -** ████ ID No./Dist ████	I N F	Returnable Court Date	Returnable Court Time	( ) A.M. ( ) P.M.
Sworn and subscribed before me the undersigned authority This **5** day of **November** **2009**	O R M A T I O N	Release Date	Release Time	( ) A.M. ( ) P.M.
SIGNATURE of Person Authorized to Administer Oath ████		Releasing Officer		
████ PRINTED Name/Title of Person Authorized to Administer Oath		Page **2** of Page **3**		

A - 3

11/06/2009 Filed Lee County Clerk of Courts-Criminal Division

NARRATIVE/CONTINUATION

	1 Offense	Juvenile	1 Original
	2 Arrest 2		2 Supplement

ADM

Agency ORI Number	Agency Name	Agency Report Number
FL████████	**Lee County Sheriff's Office**	█████████
Original Date Reported **10/29/2009**	Case Reference	

Detective ████ spoke with ████████████ who stated Michael Angelo Cinelli had come to her residence this date. He turned over a necklace, pendant and her husbands gold bracelet. This is the same property description as what was received by Michael Angelo Cinelli this date from ████

Detective ████ met with Michael Angelo Cinelli at the ████ Sheriff's Office ████████ Michael Angelo Cinelli signed a rights waiver affidavit and provided a sworn taped statement. Michael Angelo Cinelli confessed to taking the property from ████████████ residence.

Based upon the evidence and statements obtained probable cause was established for the arrest of Michael Angelo Cinelli for one count of Grand Theft and Dealing in Stolen Property.

NARRATIVE / CONTINUATION

ADMINISTRATIVE

Report Contains				Related Report Number(s)			
Officer(s) Reporting **Detective -** ████████████			ID Number(s)		Unit		Date
Officer Reviewing (If Applicable)	ID Number	Routed To	Referred To	Assigned To	By	Date

Case Status **Closed**	Clearance Type 1 Arrest 2 Exceptional 3 Unfounded 1	A - Adult J - Juvenile A	Date Cleared 1 ,1 ,0 ,5 ,0 ,9	Arrest Number	Number Arrested 1
Exception Type 1 Extradition Denied 2 Arrest on Primary Offense Secondary Offense Without Prosecution 3 Death of Offender 4 V W Refused to Cooperate 5 Prosecution Denied 6 Juvenile / No Custody				OSTS Number	Page 3 of Page 3

A - 2

CHAPTER 14

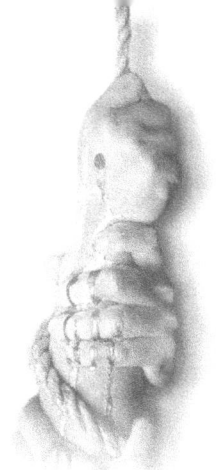

KIDNAPPED

I closed my eyes tightly. The air began to feel heavy. The cell was closing in around me. I was sure the icy metal bars would be touching my back any minute. This feeling was not unfamiliar, and I hated it.

The sounds of door buzzers and flushing toilets grated on my nerves. The smell of mildew mixed with chlorine made my stomach quiver. Hopelessness held my throat in a death grip. I opened my eyes long enough to climb to the top bunk and curl up on the thin foam mattress. Apparently, no one could find the pillow I asked for. My comfort was on no one's priority list.

I covered my head with the one thin, prickly blanket they had provided. My nose started to sting. It had been a long time since I had allowed myself to cry. There was no use trying to stop these tears. I bawled until I was gulping for air. Years of pain, rejection, failure, and shame erupted from the deepest parts of me. I cried until there was no crying left in me.

Then, for a long time, I just laid still. I concentrated on trying to make my lip stop twitching. A face kept coming up in my mind. I remembered the first time I met her. I had been at my dad's church.

A friend pulled me by the arm. "There's someone I want you to meet."

She looked at me with sincere and caring eyes. "Hi, my name is Ivette."

We had only spoken for a few moments. Something about her smile conveyed genuine acceptance. I had written my number on a piece of paper and gave it to her. We said goodbye and I left feeling pretty certain I would never hear from her.

Three days later, my phone beeped. A text. "Hi. :)"

That one-word text and smiley face had caused my heart to do a little dance of excitement. So, she was thinking of me, too. Later that night, we talked for hours. She was something special.

I tossed that memory around in my mind as I dozed. I was soon startled awake by the clanging of the door being opened.

"Cinelli, pack your stuff!" The guard was rough and tough, and he wasn't trying to hide it. "You made bail."

Wow. Dad had bailed me out again. As I walked toward the exit, I could see my dad waiting outside. He had come to take me home.

"Thank you." I couldn't believe it. My dad kept showing up. I knew I would have to face a judge for what I had done. For now, today, I was free.

"One-year probation and restitution," my lawyer explained. My freedom was in that judge's hands. "Can you pay it now?"

That was fast. No more jail time was a huge relief.

"I'll take it. I think I can pay now." My response took a lot of nerve. *I don't have a penny to my name.* I questioned my dad with a glance.

His nod confirmed he would pay it for me. With all of the business taken care of, we got in the car and headed home. It was a quiet ride back to the East Coast.

I knew I had better work on getting my life together. In a few days, a local restaurant hired me as a prep cook. I began to attend church every week.

One Sunday, the girl I had met, Ivette, passed me in the hallway. "Hey, you're back."

"Yeah. I'm working through some personal issues," I told her. I had to be vague. I wasn't ready to lose her by sharing my story too soon. There was curiosity in her eyes, but she didn't ask me questions.

"Can I take you to dinner?" I asked. Hesitantly, she said yes.

After that, we began to find every excuse to see each other. On occasion, I would surprise her for lunch. I began to think I was in love with her. It was wonderful. It was scary.

After one of those lunches, as I was headed back to my apartment, fear took over my thoughts. If she found out the whole truth, surely she would run in the other direction. Rejection seemed to be waiting behind every date, every phone call, every text. I knew I couldn't bear the pain of being rejected, but the pain of anticipating the pain of rejection was even harder to handle. Anxiety screamed louder than reason. I had to do something to quiet it. I knew what I had to do and where I had to go to do it.

I'll control it this time.

I lied to myself and believed every word. I turned my car around and drove in the direction of the one thing that had never let me down.

"This stuff always works," I tried to reassure myself. I had made a serious mistake. The word "self-sabotage" flashed before my eyes, but I couldn't feel anything.

"Pee in the cup." The probation officer stood behind me, arms folded across his chest. He didn't have all day.

I stood paralyzed at the urinal. The dingy wall in front of me was garnished with black smudges. Behind me, I could feel the officer's icy glare. I knew it would be dirty urine. I wasn't getting out of this. I took a deep breath.

"Finally." The officer took the cup I offered him with a shaky hand. "Took long enough." He dropped the test strip in.

We waited for a forever-long five minutes.

"You're dirty for opiates and cocaine." This was no news to me. I could have saved us the time it took for the test. "We have to send this to the lab to determine the levels. Someone will contact you."

It was bittersweet. I wasn't going to jail today, but I would eventually face consequences. I hurried to my car. I couldn't stop now. I had to get high before I went to work. In fact, I planned to stay high until they came to get me.

Bang, bang, bang!

I jumped up and ran to the door. The apartment was small and the neighbors lived close by. I threw the door open.

"You got my $200?" The dealer shoved his way past me. "You're coming with me."

I did owe this guy money, but I didn't have two cents. The guy was waving something around in his hand. I panicked when I realized it was a knife. He wasn't kidding. I sidled slowly toward the door. My mind frantically searched for a way to escape.

"Where's my $200?!" He was shouting now.

The neighbors must be hearing this.

He was angrily jabbing his finger at my face. He raised his arm and swung hard, his long fingernail slicing into my eye. The pain nearly floored me. Both of my eyes began to tear up until everything was blurry. I couldn't let this guy see my fear. Then, he grabbed my arm, dragged me out, and shoved me into the back seat of a car. "Give me your driver's license. Close your eyes. Don't look at me."

I stared at the floor. He jumped into the passenger seat. The driver hit the gas and sped away. My death loomed before me as a very real possibility. We drove around in silence for what felt like hours.

"I don't have any money. I can pay you when I get my check." That sounded lame even to me.

"Then you better call someone. I better get my money tonight." His words were sinister, just like in the movies. Only worse, these kidnappers weren't acting.

Since it was after midnight, the list of people I could call was short. I knew of only one person. We worked together at my last job. Hoping he was still awake, I took the phone the dealer held out.

"Hey, I can't really tell you the whole story right now, but I'm in trouble. Can you leave $200 in cash at my apartment?" I hoped I sounded normal.

"What is it for? Why? Are you in trouble? What's happening?" This was not an unreasonable response.

"I can't get into that right now. Please. I will pay you back. Can you please go there?"

I guess he knew me well enough to take me seriously. "I will drop it off in forty-five minutes."

I felt the muscles in my neck and shoulders loosen slightly. I realized I had been holding my breath.

What happens now?

"We'll go by your apartment and check in forty-five minutes." The dealer was literally snarling. "Your friend had better come through."

Oh, you don't want him to come through as much as I want him to.

An addict can't ignore his addiction for long. I was in a car with two unscrupulous drug dealers, fearing for my very life, but

I just wanted to get high. Maybe my friend would leave more than $200.

How low are you willing to go? Shame made me shake my head as I tried to stop these thoughts. *Just how desperate are you?*

My next thought answered that question. *Maybe these guys will front me for more drugs after they get their money.*

My eye was swollen and oozing a reddish liquid. It hurt badly. The driver parked at my apartment. From somewhere deep inside my broken self, I rallied the debatable courage to ask, "Will you front me a twenty-dollar rock?"

The dealer looked at me with something that might have resembled pity. "Nah, go get more money."

The two men had gotten what they came for. I slunk into my bed, disgrace and humiliation accompanying me. My eye was swollen shut. I felt sick and disgusting. I vowed I would never tell a soul about what happened that night.

It had been two months since I skipped out on probation. Worry threatened to crush me. My phone rang. "Hey, Dad."

"The probation officer called. He said the police have a warrant for your arrest. I'm coming to pick you up."

I jumped up and got dressed. I walked down the street so I wouldn't be at the apartment if the police came. I hopped into the passenger seat of my dad's car.

"You have to turn yourself in." It was a matter of fact.

"I know, Dad. Can we stall for a few hours?"

Dad agreed and drove us to the beach. We parked and began to walk on the beach. Dad suggested getting ice cream. Sitting outside drinking chocolate milkshakes felt unfamiliarly normal. The smell of the ocean and the cool of the breeze refreshed my soul. I was loving these moments with my dad.

Dad's phone rang. It was the manager of the apartment building. The two talked for a few minutes. I tried to swallow the lump in my throat as my chest tightened. This was serious. They were looking for me and they wouldn't stop until they found me.

"The police searched your apartment."

I was beginning to feel the detox coming on. My skin felt like insects were crawling over and under it. I was feeling sick and began shivering, trying to get warm. Minutes later, sweat beaded on my forehead and dripped off my nose because I felt so hot. My eyes and nose spewed liquid. Nausea followed. I had to admit defeat.

"Dad, I will turn myself in. First, will you take me to my friend's house?"

He didn't ask me any questions. He drove me there. I ran inside and got two Suboxone pills from my buddy. Suboxone is a drug that is used to manage the symptoms of withdrawal from other opiates. I had no idea how long I would be incarcerated. Being sick in jail painted a frightening picture.

Parked at the local police station, we sat quietly in the car for several moments. I couldn't bring myself to get out. But there was no use delaying. This had to happen. It took every ounce of my will to get out of the car. Cramming the two pills under my tongue, I immediately felt the comforting warmth of the drug run through my body. I willed the pills to last long enough.

I turned back and gave my dad a big hug. "I'm sorry." These tears were real ones. Humiliation ruled the moment. "I hope I can get over this someday."

"I love you." I knew he loved me and I could hardly stand knowing it. "I will always be here for you."

We walked into the station together. "I'm here to turn myself in."

Maybe it was brave. What other choice did I have? Two officers came from down the hall. I thought the handcuffs were unnecessary. I wasn't going anywhere. I felt the cold steel on my wrists. I had heard that stomach-churning metallic click too many times already.

CHAPTER 15

JAILHOUSE ENTREPRENEUR

The officer shoved me into a cell. I was so weak and sick that I just fell to the floor. "I need to go to the infirmary." I really should have. They weren't convinced.

After being moved four times, I was escorted outside to a waiting police transport truck. "Where am I going?"

"You're being extradited to Fort Myers."

Curled up on the icy steel truck floor, I felt the handcuffs dig into my wrists. The pain kept my mind off the misery of detoxing. Two and a half hours of bouncing around allowed for very little sleep.

"Get out." They had quite the welcoming committee.

Barely functioning, I did my best to just do as I was told. It took hours, but I eventually ended up in a bed. My pillow was a rolled-up tank top. My body was done. Sleep was a blessed relief. I don't know how long I slept.

A voice woke me. "Hey, your lawyer is here to see you."

I certainly wasn't recovered, but I got up and staggered after the officer. I was surprised to see my lawyer on the other side of the thick glass. I sat down and picked up the receiver.

"Did my dad call you?" No pleasantries were needed here. This was business.

"Yes. I've spoken to the prosecutor. They're offering you two choices. You can go back on probation and start over with two years. Or you can spend six months in jail."

This misery or that misery. You choose. "Can I think about it?"

The guy was doing his job. It seemed like maybe he cared about me. We said our goodbyes, and I was escorted back to my cell. The fact that my dad had hired the lawyer again shocked me. I was incredibly grateful.

The next day I went to court, attired in an orange jumpsuit and accessorized with shiny metal wrist and ankle shackles. I felt insignificant in the middle of the huge courtroom.

My answer to the lawyer was certain. "I'll take the six months in jail." I didn't trust myself to stay clean.

The gavel struck the sound block. I could hear its echo as I was ushered away. With good behavior, I would spend the next 153 days confined to a jail cell in the drug rehabilitation wing.

As I had done so many times before, I decided to make the best of my time in confinement. I read the Bible. I prayed. I began to search my heart for purpose and meaning. I tried to imagine being like Jesus.

"Do not let kindness and truth leave you; bind them around your neck, write them on the tablet of your heart. So you will find favor and a good reputation in the sight of God and man" (Prov. 3:3-4 NASB). This Bible verse encouraged me and inspired me to stick to my plan.

Every weekday, a drug counselor came into the jail and conducted lessons with the inmates. I desired to learn and grow. I asked questions. I listened to the feedback. The idea of being genuine and kind spurred me on. Soon, other inmates began to respect me and listen to me.

The counselor eventually asked me to share my story in front of a group of inmates. Hesitantly, I agreed. I was sure these guys would laugh at me. What could I possibly say to them?

I prayed. I began to write my thoughts. "Knowing the Voice of God" emerged as the title of my talk. The next day, I stood before these men who were just like me. Addicted. Confused. Ashamed. Unable to overcome. At first, I stumbled over my words. Then I saw their eyes focused on me. They were listening. They wanted to hear hope. Their response grew my faith. I became a part of the "in crowd."

"Hey, can I trade two lunch trays for two honey buns?" I asked a guy in the lunch line.

He didn't have to think long. "Yeah, I'll do that."

Without commissary money from my family, I couldn't get extra food or snacks. Why not start a store?

I spread the word that I would be operating a one-for-two store. I loaned out one honey bun or other item and, when a fellow inmate received commissary money from his family, he paid me back two items. It became a well-established business with a full inventory of assorted pastries, candy bars, and chips. Being the "President" of inmates didn't exactly qualify as a high honor, but I was excited to gain that title. I began to believe that God really loved me and was intent on blessing me. Daily changes were taking place in my heart.

At the same time, I was inspired to write poetry. Apparently, I was good at it. The guys found out and began to buy my poems to send to their loved ones. Even the drug counselor asked me to write a poem for her. I still have a letter she wrote letting me know how much the poem had meant to her.

Five months sailed by. My last night in jail finally came. Since I still had an inventory of goodies, I decided we should have a party. We had a great time eating "jailhouse cakes" and burritos together.

"Cinelli!"

I thought I was dreaming. I heard my name again. It was real.

"You're being released."

The clock said 3:00 a.m. I grabbed all my belongings—just a manilla folder stuffed with important papers. I traded my red jumpsuit for the same clothes I had worn when my dad and I drank milkshakes together. What a feeling to walk out of that gate.

Dad was waiting for me. We hugged. No matter how many times I needed help, my dad was there—even in the wee hours of the morning. I was humbled. We climbed into his car and headed east. I couldn't contain the excitement I felt to be getting another fresh start.

CHAPTER 16

RUNNING FOR MY LIFE

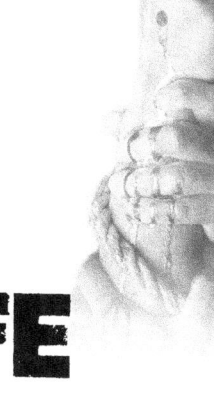

"You need to get help."

This wasn't the first time I had heard my dad say those words. I was so sick. I had no money. Addicts don't have action plans besides how they will get their next high.

How in the world had I let this happen again?

"Are you really going to go tomorrow?"

I had agreed to go to another year-long rehab program. I would be leaving in the morning. "Yes. I am going." At least I planned to keep my word. "I need $100 to get me through the night."

I knew I was asking my dad to make an agonizing decision to break the unspoken rule—don't enable an addict by providing cash. This time, it was the means to an end. We both knew that if I was sick and detoxing, I would refuse to go.

I shuffled through the kitchen, stopping to get a drink of water. Back in the bedroom, I spotted the $100 bill on the bed. Relief and regret traveled through my body. I regretted making him choose. I hopped in my car and sped as fast as I could to Miami where I procured a bundle of heroin. That equated to ten one-dose baggies. Buy ten and get two free with my dealer. I was desperate to avoid the sickness of detox.

Deep shame rode with me all the way back to my dad's house. The sickness was gone. I felt normal. I had been doing well. A reputable insurance agency had given me a great job. I was making money. Ivette and I were still connecting. We had enjoyed a few dates. But I didn't deserve any of that. I knew it was short-lived anyway. I would lose it all sooner than later. The pressure was unbearable. It was easier to just get high.

In the morning, I grabbed my duffle bag of possessions and jumped into the car with my dad.

Loser. Failure. Loser. Failure.

I was having one-track thoughts. We were silent the entire drive. Dad dropped me off at the facility and left. He was probably done with me anyway.

A month into the program, someone asked me if I would like to work in the kitchen. The rehab program was sponsored by a large church. They had a restaurant on campus. My kitchen experience at Teen Challenge would be useful. I had also done a stint delivering pizzas and helping in a pizza restaurant. That was good enough for them. They told me to report to the restaurant a couple of days later. I wasn't a skilled cook, but I was not afraid to try it out.

The manager introduced himself. "What station can you work?"

That made me nervous. *What is a station?* "I've helped on sauté before."

"Perfect. We need a sauté chef."

I decided to work hard and learn as much as I could. I memorized the recipes. I followed each step precisely. I paid close attention to the taste and quality of the food. The opportunity to be free and creative inspired me. I felt like God was close to me every moment. Soon, the head chef took notice and began teaching me and giving me more responsibilities.

My year in the rehab program was coming to an end. I didn't have a plan going forward. My skills were few except for what I had learned about restaurant kitchens. There was only one place where hope made sense. I decided to surrender my life to the Lord, at least to the best of my ability.

A few weeks after I graduated, the restaurant hired me for a full-time position. I was super excited to have a job. I felt like God saw me and was working on my behalf. Ivette was still sticking by me. I moved into a house with other graduates of the program. We had many perks, including a TV. I was ready to face a new chapter in my life. How could things get any better?

In fact, things were going so well that I began to forget about God. Excuses became regular as I told myself, "I'll just skip prayer and devotions today. I'll make it up tomorrow." Tomorrow never came. Days turned into weeks. The depression crept back into my heart and soul.

I got this. I'll be fine. I won't ever use drugs again. I wanted to keep this promise. But I couldn't stop thinking about the void and the deep pain in my chest. Fear terrorized my thoughts. I had to make this stop.

I thought I had become a Christian. *Should I be having these struggles?* Hey, I had been baptized! I remembered that night vividly.

Our church held Friday night Bible studies in the homes of congregants. I was sitting in the middle of the room. I wasn't really paying attention. I was only ten years old. The man who was teaching casually asked if anyone wanted to get baptized. After an hour of not listening, those were the only words I heard. Mysteriously, the muscles in my shoulder and arm came alive and my hand shot up in the air. The next thing I knew, I was clad in a bathing suit and about to be dunked in the pool.

"I baptize you in the name of the Father, the Son, and the Holy Spirit." Whatever other words were said were muffled as my ears were submerged under the water. Well, I didn't feel any different. In my heart, I knew this was important. I knew it signified Jesus' resurrection. I hoped He was watching.

Surely God would step in at any moment and make big changes in my life.

I began to go to the gym regularly. I was taking vitamin supplements to perk me up. They didn't work. I watched movies and played video games until I wanted to explode. No distraction was working. I needed more. One persistent thought won over all the others.

I'll just see if there might be anyone around who is selling drugs.

I jumped on my bike and rode through the neighborhood looking for someone to give me "the nod." I rode for hours.

I think that guy just nodded at me.

As I watched, the guy ducked behind a convenience store. I rode around to meet him. "You got that boy?"

"Nah, I got rock and Dilaudid." He seemed to know I would take whatever he had.

My stomach churned. I could taste the regret. "Let me get a forty rock and two Dilaudid." I grabbed the crack rock and narcotics and high-tailed it out of there.

I pedaled as fast as my legs would allow. Anticipation heightened all of my senses. Back home, behind the locked bathroom door, the sizzle of the crack rock seemed loud, but I didn't care. Instead of calm, anxiety and paranoia took control of my body. My ears were ringing. I dissolved one of the Dilaudid pills in water, loaded a syringe, and jabbed the needle into my arm. The tip of the old needle was dull. It needed a hard jab. *Pop.* Blood seeped into the syringe. I pressed the plunger with my thumb and watched the clear liquid flow into my vein. My body relaxed. A metallic taste filled my mouth. I was calm. Numb. Worry and pain melted away. I snuck out of the bathroom and slid under the covers.

Hope everyone is asleep. I was out like a light.

Daylight. Familiar voices rang in my head and remorse vibrated in the pit of my stomach.

Failure. Loser.

Accusation. Condemnation. Shame. *How did I get here again?*

The ringing phone startled me. Ivette. *I can't answer. She can't ever know. She will never talk to me again.* Ignoring the phone, I headed off to work. *That was the absolute last time. I won't do that again.*

I made it two whole days.

Despair is an intense feeling of hopelessness. Despair filled my heart and filled my soul. I grabbed my bike and started on a mission: find the guy.

"There he is," I said out loud. Same convenience store. Same exchange.

"Hey, take my number. You won't have to ride around." He was more than happy to make it easier for me to give him my money.

I typed his number on my phone. *Huh. Under "D" for dealer?*

I managed to hide my drug use for several more weeks.

Eventually, the paranoia from the drugs was close to unmanageable. I cleared a space under the bed. Squeezing underneath, I surrounded myself with my empty suitcases. I stayed there smoking crack for hours. Sweat poured out of my body. I seriously needed water. Just as I was about to slide out, I heard the doorknob jiggle.

The voices of the director and another staff member filled the room. I froze, staying deadly still. The weight of my entire body was pressing on my elbow. It hurt. I could see the men's shoes. If I was found, they would call the police. *Not good.* After an eternity of shaking and straining, I was thrilled to hear them leave the room. I slid out from my hiding place, slipped outside, grabbed my bike, and rode as fast and as far as I could. I texted the director and lied to him. I would be staying at my dad's house that night.

What I really did was go straight to a hotel and rent a room.

The next day, after a shower and some clean clothes, I rode back to the house. I felt confident that I had duped everyone. I saw a few people casually hanging around outside the director's office.

See, no one knows. I would check to see what was happening. I was feeling good. I had saved one Dilaudid for the next morning.

"What's going on, guys?" I tried to act cool as I walked through the reception area. Then I noticed the room seemed oddly full of people . . . The program director and some of the students were sitting around a desk. The director looked straight at me, and I knew. I knew he knew. I was high and still hoping no one would notice. It was his *job* to notice.

"Let's go into my office." My roommate must have told him I was locking myself in the bathroom all night.

"Sure, no problem." It's hard to sound confident when you're as guilty as I was.

In the director's office, he got right to the point. "Have you been using?"

I'm sure my face went white. My mind surely went blank. "No way!"

The director kept prying. "So, if you are clean, you won't mind taking a drug test?"

Lying seemed useful here. A drug test would seal my fate. "Well, I did use once. Like two days ago." This was it. One last plea. "Please, don't kick me out. I don't have anywhere to go."

Judging from the look he gave, I'm pretty sure the director was disgusted with me. "Wait outside while I discuss this situation with the other leaders."

This would be bad news. I was about to be back out there again.

"We're not willing to walk this journey with you anymore." The wound of rejection I had been trying to heal with all the drugs was ripped wide open.

Here I go again. I got up to walk out of the office. They asked me to wait a few minutes so they could call my dad. I just kept walking. I grabbed my duffle bag from my room and jumped on my bike.

My phone rang.

Guess they did call my dad.

"Hey, Dad, can I come home?" I told him all about the last few weeks. He had always been there for me. This was getting ridiculous, and I knew it.

"No, but if you can find a halfway house that will take you, I'll help you get in." I might have heard compassion in his voice.

Hours went by. I made phone calls. No one wanted to help. Fear gripped me as I realized I'd be sleeping in an alley again. The vibration of the phone surprised me. It was a friend who was the director of a rehab program.

"I have a halfway house that would be willing to take you. You'll need to have a clean drug test in three days. Can you do that?"

I hesitated. I wasn't sure I was ready to stop using drugs. The need for a place to stay won that argument. "Yeah, I can do that." Relieved, I searched for a scrap of paper to write down the address.

I am a complete failure. How will I be able to stay clean?

I made it to the halfway house despite the after-effects of the drugs I had taken. The manager met me, walked me to my room, introduced me to my new roommate, and left.

It was an old, run-down house. The dingy bedroom smelled musty. An old squeaky mattress was all the bed offered. No sheets, no blankets. I fished a sweater out of the small bag holding my only worldly possessions. It was a depressing reminder of all I had lost. I hadn't slept in days. I curled up on the bare mattress and fell asleep.

I was startled awake by clunking and squealing noises. The ancient wall air conditioning unit was working hard. Apparently, the heat had gotten the best of it. It soon produced a high-pitched ringing sound that kept me from sleeping the rest of the night.

How can I stop using drugs if I have to live in a place like this?

I stared at the ceiling as my skin began to crawl. The drug obsession slithered over my body like a boa constrictor getting ready to squeeze. My mind was screaming at me.

You have no choice. You have to get high. YOU FAILURE!

Stomach churning, body shaking all over, I tip-toed out the back door and grabbed my bike. I pedaled fast.

"I hope that guy is there." I think I spoke the words out loud. I had to get what I needed and get back to the house before anyone knew I was gone.

"There he is." Out loud again.

He looked my way and our eyes locked. Anticipation hit me like a lightning bolt. I bought as many Dilaudid as my meager dollars would cover. I crept into the house through the back door. Grabbing a spoon from the kitchen, I locked myself in the bathroom. I crushed the first pill and filled a syringe.

Boom! Boom! Boom!

"Mike, what are you doing in there?" The house manager was looking for me.

"I'm using the bathroom." I was working hard to speak in a normal voice. I had to get this shot in my arm.

Pop! I hit the vein. Blood spurted into the syringe like a little red cloud. Adrenaline spurred me to act quickly. I pushed the plunger hard and pulled it out.

"Got it," I whispered to myself. I stuffed the drugs and paraphernalia into my shoe. The manager would ask me to empty my pockets. I unlocked the door, and the manager shoved it open. We stood face-to-face.

"Did you leave and come back?"

"No, I haven't left."

"Empty your pockets."

I placed my keys, wallet, and cell phone on the kitchen counter. "That's all I have," I lied.

"You will have a drug test in two days. You had better be clean." He walked away, most likely suspecting I wouldn't be. My heart pounded. I had conned him this time. Next time might be a different story.

Test day came. On the way to work, I bought a detox drink from a gas station. I hoped it would get me through this drug test. Last time, I drank a cap-full of bleach and chased it down with an energy drink, but that had no effect. When I returned to the house after work, the manager was waiting for me. The drink worked and I passed. Still, I hadn't learned anything. I was getting sick again from detoxing. I had to get high.

It didn't matter that I had passed the test. A few days later, I was back on the streets. The manager had had enough. I couldn't stop using.

I guess I'll just go harder. This is familiar.

A week later, I was hiding in a hotel room. I owed a drug dealer money. Paranoid. Sick. Dehydrated. I couldn't hit a vein anymore. My arms were swollen, hard bumps forming over each place I missed the vein. Infection was a huge possibility.

I gotta get out of here.

I called my dad again. I got into another halfway house. I was still using. Hiding in the closet, I smoked crack while blood ran down my arm after I shot myself up with heroin. I couldn't understand why I was so miserable. I couldn't begin to fathom the abyss of pain that was controlling me. I couldn't confront it without the drugs.

There was so much pain. There were so many memories I couldn't face. Like May 10th and June 12th. My mother's birthday and her death day. Throw Mother's Day into the middle of that. I couldn't face thinking about how my dad had abandoned me and my mother's memory by giving his love to another woman. I couldn't face the loss of all my ex-girlfriends and the love I so desperately craved. Most of all, I couldn't face the shocking things I had done while under the influence of the demonic control of crack cocaine and the junkies' needles. I could not face the shame that came from the awful things I had done, nor the shame of the things that had been done to me that were not my choice. If I stayed numb, I would never have to face any of these memories.

I can't stop. I won't stop.

I was kicked out again. I called my dad. "Dad, I'm in trouble again. I have nowhere to go."

Thirty seconds of silence.

"There is a place I found for you to go. If you want to go there, you have to call them yourself."

"Okay, I'll call right now." I made the call and talked to the pastor who answered. This time, it was in Chattanooga, Tennessee. I didn't want to move again. I had moved way too many times. Would I ever have a place I could call home?

The pastor assured me he had one bed available if I wanted it. I told him I was coming. I wanted to go. But still, my addiction was calling the shots. My brain disengaged from any logic. It was easier to keep getting high because I didn't want to go through coming down and feeling sick. I knew what was waiting for me if I stopped. At least this way, I could stay numb. Within minutes, I had called some people and went on a binge.

"Mike, what are you doing in there?"

I was locked in the bathroom. Someone was banging on the door. A familiar moment. I had been awake for four or five days. I couldn't remember exactly how long. *Where am I anyway?*

I didn't know the last time I had showered or changed my clothes. Paranoia from sleep deprivation and crack cocaine usage was taking its toll. I was hallucinating.

I opened the door a bit and said I would be out in a minute. I loaded a syringe with the heroin I had purchased with my last few dollars. I had to come down from this high.

Memories from the last week began to surface. I had asked for an advance on my paycheck and then stopped showing up to work. My hope was that I would just not wake up one morning. With a couple of other guys, I rented a sleazy hotel room in a drug-infested area of town. One of the guys sold crack from the room. I needed a place to keep getting high.

Finally, I got the courage to walk out of the bathroom. "Let me get a forty on credit?"

The dealer was watching me stagger to the bed. "Nah bro, you already owe me forty."

I knew it was over. In a few hours, I would be very sick. I had nothing left to make any deals.

"Hey, bro, I need to do laundry. Can you drop me at the laundromat?" I was attempting to look and sound confident. I knew this guy was all about his money and would be demanding it soon. I was looking for a way to escape. Having been kidnapped once already, I was not looking for any more trouble.

"Alright. I'll drop you off and I'll pick you up in one hour. I'm gonna collect what you owe."

I grabbed my duffle bag and hopped out of the car. I shuffled inside without looking back. As soon as I saw the car drive away, I ran. Straight to my dad's house. My only rational thought was that I hoped the pastor was still saving that bed for me.

I knocked on the door. My stepmom answered. She didn't look too happy to see me.

"Is dad home? They're coming for me in an hour. I need to go. To get out of here."

She explained that my dad wasn't there.

I begged her to get him on the phone.

The phone rang. It had to be my deliverance. "Dad, I'm sorry to do this to you. I owe them money. They're coming back for me. Can we leave for that place in Chattanooga?"

Dad sounded noticeably frustrated. Still, he assured me he was on his way.

Back in my old bathroom at my dad's house, I slowly peeled the stiff fabric, once referred to as my clothing, off my filthy body. It may have been two or three weeks since I stepped into a shower or even changed my clothes. The putrid smell of sweat mixed with the toxins of the heroin and cocaine oozed out of my pores. My fingertips were raw and scabbed over from incessantly picking my skin—a side effect of the drugs. Swelling and bruising decorated my arms from shoulder to wrist. Dull needles jabbed into the skin had left their telltale marks. My tongue and the insides of my cheeks were raw and festering from the constant grinding of my teeth. The shower was relief and agony mingled together. Anxiety threatened to be the end of me. I cried out to God.

"Where are You?!"

 Giving recognition to the tears and anguish would do me no good. I swallowed hard and kept on moving. That dealer would not stop looking for me. Finally in clean clothes, I threw my meager possessions into the car. Dad and I drove off. Starting over. Again. Fear encompassed my body and mind. Sleep was pounding at each of my senses. I hadn't slept in five or six days.

As we left Broward County, a peace came over me and I went to sleep.

CHAPTER 17

CHATTANOOGA

I was headed to another residential program. Another year would be spent institutionalized. This was the third long-term rehab out of a list of many. I wondered if a normal life would ever be possible.

Will I someday have a family? A good, stable job? I have a dreadful credit score. My debt is beyond any hope of ever being paid off. The one girl I thought could love me had given up on me. I am nothing but a loser, a failure. I will never be good enough.

I woke up to these disturbing thoughts. Then, I consoled myself with a great solution.

I know how to survive on the streets. As soon as my dad drops me off, I'll just leave.

I had never been to Chattanooga, Tennessee. I had no idea where I was. After gulping down a burger and smoking my last cigarette, we headed to the address. We pulled into a large parking lot.

It was a church. Together, we went inside.

"Hey there, are you Mike?" asked a friendly voice.

"Yeah." My voice was muffled and slurred. I was embarrassed and quite sick. I desperately needed to lay down.

Why can't I stop doing this over and over?

As the guy politely droned on about the program to which I was about to agree and what would be expected of me, I sat still and pretended to listen. In reality, I heard nothing he said. I was fully focused on one thought.

How can I get away from here and get high?

After what seemed like hours to me, I was taken to the facility across the street and directed to the room where I would live for the next twelve months. Top bunk again.

I am thirty-two years old. I should definitely not be sleeping on the top bunk in another rehab facility with only a small duffle bag full of scanty possessions to call my own. I give up.

"God, if You really see me, will You please help me?" I spoke the words out loud. I was wretchedly sick and devoid of any smidgen of hope. I made what felt like a deathbed deal. "God, I will commit to staying here and making this work. If You will change my heart . . . change my mind . . . change my thinking."

Over the next weeks and months, I did see my life begin to change. The cooking skills I had gained from previous rehab programs served me well. Part of this program's recovery process was to provide jobs for the residents. I was able to work at the church's cafe, and began to build meaningful and caring relationships. These people listened to me. I started to believe God had a plan for me and I could become the man He had intended me to be. The idea of forgiveness became a real and attainable goal. My soul was overflowing with bitterness and resentment toward my family and everyone I had ever loved. I realized I had been drowning in the effects of trauma my whole life. It seemed like I had just come up for air.

Three months after entering the program, I met a guy named Al. I was pretty sure God had something to do with this man coming into my life. He became my mentor and took me under his wing. One day, Al came to the church to have lunch with me. As we sat at the table, he asked, "Have you checked your credit report recently?"

Really? What did that have to do with anything?

I shook my head. I did not want to think about that. I had student loan debt, credit card bills, and old medical bills. Collection agencies from all over were looking for me.

Al wasn't going to let it go. "You can use my computer any time you want to print out the report."

I was a bit startled at the foreboding sense of responsibility that began to spread over me. I was having a revelation: I needed to work on fixing this.

I told Al that I would like to use his computer, and I printed out over 150 pages which showed the ugly results of my years of irresponsibility. I was determined to dig myself out of this mess. Over the next six months, I attended a financial coaching class. For the first time ever, I began to understand how a budget worked and began to use one. I started the long journey of paying off the huge debts I had accumulated over the years of living in my addiction. Responsibility was feeling amazingly good.

By this time, the holidays were fast approaching. I looked forward to going back to Florida to see my family and had even saved up some money for a plane ticket. A week before I was set to leave, I received a phone call from an old friend.

"Hi, Mike. I heard you were coming down to Florida. Would you want to share your story at a recovery meeting while you're here?"

Wow, this guy knew my whole story. All the long years of it. I guessed he must think I had something worthwhile to say. I quickly told him I would love to do that. It was exciting to have the opportunity.

On the day of the recovery meeting, I was nervous. I would be standing in front of a crowd of people. When I saw Ivette walk through the door, my nervousness sky-rocketed. We had not spoken in a very long time. She knew I was struggling with addiction, but I was sure she didn't understand the real impact that it had on my life. I thought I had lost her. In fact, our last conversation was a big fight about my addiction and the fact that I was always disappearing. Then I disappeared again to Chattanooga.

After the meeting, I headed for the door. Ivette was walking out at the same time. Our eyes met. It looked like maybe she still had feelings for me. I had certainly thought about her every day we were apart.

"Could we go get coffee tomorrow?" It was a risk. Surprisingly, her answer was yes. I was so excited that I barely slept all night. My mind raced.

If she and I are together, how will it work? Could I move back to Florida? Will it be a good idea to leave the program where I'm doing so well? I decided to relax and hoped God would get involved in the decisions. I had been learning to try to trust Him to help me with my life.

Ivette and I met for coffee the next day. It was as if our connection had never been broken. She was committed to following Jesus Christ. We both confessed to each other that we wanted whatever God wanted for our lives. I sincerely hoped He wanted Ivette to be a part of mine. That date began a new chapter in our relationship and in my life.

Chattanooga had been good for me. Having friends, being part of a church family, and being able to stay away from drugs gave me confidence. I was growing more mature in my thoughts and my actions, and I was experiencing healing in my mind and my body every day. My need to use drugs was becoming an increasingly distant memory. A normal life finally looked like a real possibility.

Over the next few months, Ivette came to visit me in Chattanooga. She brought friends or family each time. We were in love. We had been talking about the possibility of her moving to Chattanooga. The third time she came to visit, I had a special surprise. I planned to propose.

I called my dad to let him know I was ready to have my mom's engagement ring. She had left it to me to give to the person I would someday marry. This was the ring I'm sure the Lord prevented me from pawning all those years ago.

I spent a lot of time planning this big event. Ivette would be coming for my birthday so that would be my cover story. We would go out to celebrate. Then, I would pop the question. Some of my friends agreed to help.

It was perfect! I made a large wood-framed sign saying, "Will you marry me?" and attached lights to it. I had my friends place the sign on the ground below a walking bridge. I took flowers and a card to the restaurant where we would eat dinner. I wanted Ivette to know how much I loved and appreciated her. The personal touches would surely make her feel special. I even hired friends to be the camera crew to follow us and record it all. We had a great dinner. Then, I suggested walking on the path that would lead us to the bridge. When we came into view of the sign, I got down on one knee and asked the question.

She said yes!

As I placed the ring on her finger, I explained to her, "This is my mom's engagement ring. She would be so happy to know you are wearing it."

A crowd of people had gathered near the sign below us. There was cheering and clapping. It was exactly as I had hoped. I was beyond elated.

I was more than a little scared.

CHAPTER 18

JUST MARRIED

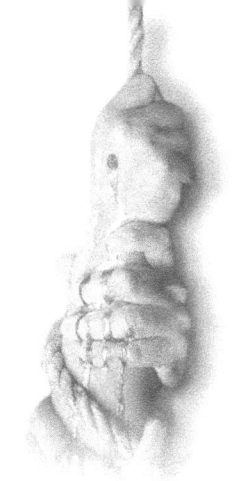

Ivette and I set a date. We were to be married in Florida in January of the following year. Ivette quit her job of ten years and moved to Chattanooga in October, so she could get settled in. I wanted so much to buy a house, but my credit score was still not good enough, not to mention my income would not support owning a home. I rented a one-bedroom apartment for her. After the wedding, I would move in.

Our wedding was beautiful, fun, and exactly how Ivette had envisioned it would be. There were no drugs and no drama. It was pure joy with so many friends and family members loving and supporting us. Afterward, we honeymooned in Cancun.

Ivette and I returned to our little one-bedroom apartment and began to settle into married life. I was working at the church cafe, and she was searching for a job. A couple of weeks after we got back, I had been asked to interview for a job as the dining services manager at an assisted living facility. I got the job. This meant I was working two full-time jobs, and in the evenings, I was detailing cars. On my one day off, I mowed lawns. I was determined to pay off my debts and build my credit. In April, Ivette finally secured a job also.

One of our dreams had always been to purchase a home together. We had saved up some money, so about four months after we were married, we decided to try again. We found a great three-bedroom home with a finished basement that had a bathroom and a separate entrance through the garage. On the day of the closing, our realtor was unable to attend so he sent a coworker in his place. As we waited for the paperwork, this woman began to tell us about Airbnb. She explained how easy it was to get started. We could rent the space in the basement and earn some extra money.

After closing on the house, Ivette and I immediately decided to research and learn all we could about how Airbnb worked. It looked like a great opportunity. We moved all the furniture we had into the basement and turned it into a quaint and comfortable studio apartment. The only piece of furniture we kept for ourselves was our bed, hoping that sacrificing the rest of our furniture would pay off. We posted pictures and listed our basement on the Airbnb website. Three days later, we had the place rented for two weeks. It didn't take us long to realize this was a worthwhile business model. We had created our first business just eight months after we were married. We named it Reinvented Concepts, LLC.

Within a few months of forming the business, we had opportunities to purchase more property. We borrowed money and bought two additional rental properties before the end of that year. Our business grew like wildfire. We bought more houses, fixed them up, and resold them for good profit. I began to involve investors and partners. Ivette and I were both still working full time—we would each take turns cleaning the Airbnbs on our lunch breaks. I was also continuing in my side jobs. On top of that, we were newlyweds trying to figure out marriage together.

Thirteen months into our marriage, it seemed like everything was going very well. Only it wasn't. Business skills I had never realized I possessed were in full bloom. However, my emotional coping skills were not. I had been clean from drugs for five years and I had received some counseling, but I was not ready for this overload. I was becoming increasingly overwhelmed. After taking on two more investors who were my friends and mentors, I became distraught. I was struggling to keep track of everything on my own. I began to isolate myself. I was shutting down. I was burned out. It had been a long time since I had felt this alone. I couldn't even share my difficulties with the men I might have spoken to before because we were now in business together.

I needed relief. I had heard about something called Kratom. Kratom is an herbal extract that comes from the leaves of an evergreen tree that grows in Asia. It's known to have an opiate effect on the body, but it's an herbal extract, so that meant it's not really a drug, right? I would try it just to help me get through these problems.

How bad could it be?

I began to live two separate lives. In front of people, I was a committed staff member at a popular, growing church. In my heart and soul, I was suffering. There seemed to be no one I could talk to about my dilemma. Since I was so involved in the church, I shouldn't be in this kind of trouble. These struggles were part of my past. I was ashamed. I couldn't tell Ivette the truth. How could she understand?

The Kratom wasn't the answer. I began to drive around bad neighborhoods where I imagined I might find drugs, but I didn't have any luck. I had heard that you could buy drugs online and have them mailed to your house.

Why not?

I started researching. It wasn't going to be easy. Using a VPN to go on the "dark web" and taking a few other precautions, I was able to place my first order. The week the drugs arrived, my parents were visiting us from Florida. I sat outside on the front porch waiting for the mailman. There were no tracking numbers involved in this kind of shipment. After several days, a package arrived. I grabbed it.

Trying to look and act halfway normal, I announced that I was going to take a nap and ran upstairs.

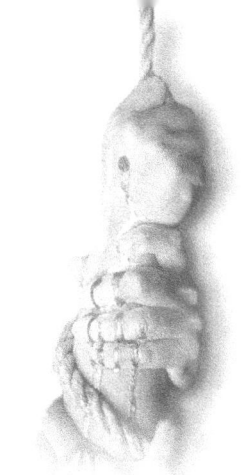

CHAPTER 19

DETOX AND FOND MEMORIES

My stomach was churning while anxiety burned my throat. I closed the door behind me and fished one of the syringes out of the box. The cocaine melted perfectly in the water, and I loaded the first shot. I paused. I hadn't used drugs for almost five years.

This is going to be bad. Here goes.

I shoved the needle into my vein and saw the cloud of blood. Relief. My face went numb. The familiar metallic taste and the warmth that accompanied it seemed to shoot through my whole body. Paranoia began.

I have to do another one.

The same sensations flooded me.

Ivette will be home any minute. I have to come down.

I melted down a small amount of the heroin in water and loaded up the syringe. It was black as tar and smelled just like it. I didn't care. I drew the dark liquid through a small piece of cotton torn from a cigarette filter. I hit the vein. My body went weak. The adrenaline from the cocaine kept me standing.

Whoa, I did too much.

I wasn't sure how I was still standing. I decided to get in the shower. *Ivette might leave me alone if I'm in the shower.*

I heard my wife come into the bathroom. "Mike, are you okay?" She poked her head through the shower curtain.

I was lying in the bathtub trying to hide the drugs. I couldn't get up and had to vomit. My vomit was black, which scared me.

"Are you okay?" Her concern was laced with anger. She knew.

I tried to convince her, *and me*, that I was fine. I just needed to rest.

I couldn't sleep. I tossed and turned all night, and tried to use the bathroom a few times. The physical pain was excruciating. This time, the physical pain beat the emotional pain.

I might need to see a doctor.

The next morning when I finally peed, it was also black. Ivette was insisting I go to the hospital, but all I could think was, *how in the world did I get here again?* I got dressed and headed for the car. I couldn't bear facing my dad. But there he was. There was only concern in his eyes. We rushed to the ER.

It wasn't immediately apparent what was wrong with me. They had drawn blood and taken urine, and we were awaiting results. Suddenly, a doctor burst through the door.

"He's in kidney failure. We need to get him on fluids, now."

I was rushed into another room. It took several attempts to get the catheter into my vein. The telltale track marks were obvious. They connected the saline solution. The doctor explained they hoped the fluids would send the numbers down and my kidneys would begin to work on their own again.

They kept me overnight. My parents sent out prayer requests to family and friends. It looked serious. The next morning, the medical team took more blood. The lab report came back within an hour. It was urgent.

"We need to put you on dialysis immediately so your kidneys can take a break."

My creatinine levels were going out of control. If this wasn't stopped, I could have permanent damage. Surgery was unavoidable. They needed to place a stent in my jugular vein.

Lying on the cold metal table in the operating room, I counted backward. *Ten, nine, eight* . . . I was out. My next memory was waking up in a recovery room alone.

How did this happen?

I was buried in remorse. The shame was ripping me apart. I could do nothing but lie there. I was helpless.

Ivette was worried about me and spent every night by my side in the hospital. I was on dialysis for five days. They monitored my creatinine levels. As the levels became more normal, they decided to see if I could go one day without dialysis. It was a miracle. The levels stayed normal. My kidneys were working!

In all, I spent eight days in the hospital. It was a frightening event. Why couldn't that stop me from what I did next?

The shame hounded me for weeks and it won. I ordered more drugs. I had to be numb. I ordered heroin. They sent me meth. I hadn't done meth before, but at this point, anything would work. I didn't want to feel anything anymore. My heart was beating with nothing but pain. I went on a three-day bender, injecting meth into my veins. I had boarded a freight train bound for disaster.

"You need to get help." Ivette was beside herself with worry. She didn't know what to do. She needed to talk to someone. If she exposed me, all we had worked so hard for would fall into ruin.

"I can't go somewhere for thirty days. We have house renovations and tenants," I argued.

"If you keep going on like this, you will die. You have to go somewhere." Sadly, she was right.

Finally, I found a place that offered a two-week detox and rehab option. I could do that. I planned to go the following week. I continued to use heroin and crack cocaine every day. I couldn't find anything to make me stop.

D-day came. *Done day?* I checked myself into the facility and was put on a regimen of Subutex, a drug used to help treat an opiate addiction. Subutex is normally administered twenty-four hours after the last use of opiates. I took it after only ten hours. I had no idea what the effects might be. Withdrawals began immediately. I was in so much pain. I thought the shame was excruciating, but there was no comparison to this. I needed to be determined.

I have to beat this. I can't give up.

Eight long, arduous days later, the withdrawal symptoms began to subside. I began to feel stronger. The two weeks went by quickly, but the chaos of my life stayed the same. I was still not prepared for the hard work it would take to finish this journey.

A few months later, I was in another rehab facility in Nashville for two weeks. It didn't seem possible, but the withdrawals were even worse this time. After one day, I was determined to leave. *Who could be expected to endure pain like this?*

A counselor intercepted my plans. She took me into her office and called Ivette. I heard her voice and broke. I didn't want to be there. But I didn't want to be sick and suffering even more. I had to make the choice.

"Please stay." I heard the tender compassion in her plea.

"Okay, babe, I will stay." I resolved to do my best. I finished the two weeks.

Keeping drugs away from addicts so they can detox is the goal of most rehab facilities. However, after long periods of drug use, the addict's brain has changed in ways that make it increasingly harder to resist the compulsions and intense urges they experience. Counseling and behavioral therapy are necessary additions to a successful treatment plan. The underlying issues that initially caused the drug use must be examined and dealt with. Most longtime addicts need to learn, or re–learn, the art of coping with negative emotions and stress. You can detox (get the drugs out of your system) in two weeks. But the process of healing your mind and body takes much longer.

I returned to the same life I left: work, financial decisions, stress. This is normal for many people, but my internal struggles were raging. The shame of what I had done, along with the merciless thoughts of failure and defeat, pounded me.

I ruin everything I touch.

Will I ever be free?

If God really cares, where is He?

I was miserable.

Well, if I'm going to be miserable, I might as well be high.

This was not exactly logical thinking. Within a couple of months, I was using heroin again. The pain from the withdrawals was bad. The pain of my past was worse. I could depend on being numb for a little while. My body was just about done. My face broke out. I couldn't sleep. I was shutting down. I refused to go to another rehab facility. I'd gone to seventeen. Going to another was impossible to imagine.

I had heard about another option. *Or maybe it was a scam?* It was called Rapid Detox. The patient is sedated with general anesthesia. Medication is administered which quickly cleans the drugs from the body. After the procedure, any residual withdrawal symptoms can be treated with medications. I was interested. Ivette researched it, as well. We found a private hospital in Florida where I could go, and the method sounded safe enough. The doctor had an excellent track record of success. We were a bit surprised to find out how expensive this option would be, but it didn't really matter. My health and our future were on the line.

I decided I needed to do this alone. However, the doctor was adamant that someone be present to help me after the procedure. I didn't want Ivette to take time off from work, so she insisted I ask my dad to come with me. I objected, but went ahead and asked him. Once again, he was willing to show up for his son. I was so thankful. I thought Dad would have given up on me by now.

Before the day of the procedure, I arranged to have one night by myself in Florida. I planned to make it worthwhile. I bought $100 of crack cocaine, crushed it into powder, and loaded it into empty capsules. I did the same with the remainder of the heroin I had on hand. I marked the capsules and put them into a pill bottle. I was only bringing a carry-on on the plane. I packed my clothes and everything I needed into the suitcase. Then, I carefully included the pill bottle full of illegal drugs.

The next morning, Ivette drove me to the airport. I was so nervous my palms were sweating. If airport security found the drugs, I would be going to jail. A fleeting thought of throwing them away was quickly dismissed by my obsession.

I'm going to take the chance.

This was a desperate move. I placed my bag on the conveyor. While my bag disappeared through the flaps of the X-ray machine, my mind was making up plausible stories just in case I was caught.

No turning back now. I walked through the metal detector.

"Excuse me, sir. We need to swab your fingers." The voice came from behind me.

I stopped breathing. I had scrubbed my nails, knowing this might happen. I had also left my belt at home, just in case there was residue on the buckle. I held my breath as they slid the swab into the machine.

The agent smiled. We waited. It seemed like an eternity.

Beep.

My heart jumped a little. The agent waved me through and bid me a good day. I finally breathed a sigh of relief, and I glanced to my right where my bag was. I made it.

A couple of hours later, I landed at the airport in Florida. Withdrawal was threatening me. I had to get to the hotel as quickly as possible. I called a taxi and recognized the hotel was half an hour away. The sick feeling in the pit of my stomach and the tightness in my chest were growing worse by the minute. When the cold chills and hot flashes began, I was in real trouble. The one thing that would make it all go away was in the bag right next to me, but I knew I couldn't take any chances. I had to get to a safe place. Putting my arm over my bag, I pulled it close.

Finally arriving at the hotel gave me great comfort. I checked in and went straight to my room. I had to get well. I couldn't bring a syringe on the plane. Snorting the drugs would be the next best thing. I poured out the contents of the pill bottle. I picked out three capsules with black marks and three without. I opened a black-marked pill. Heroin. I lined it up, rolled up a dollar bill, and snorted the smuggled powder into my nostril. Immediate relief.

I went out to get something to eat. My next stop was at the closest store where I bought a tire gauge, a copper kitchen scrubber, and a pair of scissors. I had learned to make a crack pipe using these materials.

Huh. Rather resourceful.

I created the pipe, hid it, and waited for the doctor. He stopped by the hotel room, and we reviewed the plan for the next day. Throughout the whole visit, those three capsules loaded with crack cocaine consumed my thoughts. As soon as the doctor closed the door, I was smoking. It lasted way too little time. Shame and disappointment took over as I began to come down. I had no ability to get more.

The next morning, I packed my bags and called for a taxi to take me to the hospital where I would begin my treatment. I arrived just in time for the 8:00 a.m. appointment. The rooms looked the way you imagine hospital rooms to look—plain and cold. I was having second thoughts about this. I had no idea what to expect.

"Take this and get changed." I turned around and saw the nurse handing me a paper cup of water and a small blue pill. "It will help you relax."

I accepted the water and swallowed the pill without question. I needed to relax. I recognized the blue pill. Valium. It would definitely knock off the edge of this anxiety.

The same nurse handed me a hospital gown and a diaper. *A diaper, really?* She explained it was just a precaution during the procedure.

Sheepishly, I took the gown and diaper from her. I had already committed. I was all in now. I began to feel very tired. I hadn't slept for most of the night before. I changed into the gown. And yes, I put on the diaper. My thoughts were beating me up, reminding me of the repeated failures that brought me here. Someone came in and asked me if I would like to watch TV. I think I mumbled something. My eyes were too heavy to stay open.

The next thing I knew, someone was waking me up and asking me my name. It was the doctor. There was a lot of commotion around me. Machines whirred and lights blinked. I muttered a reply and went back to sleep.

"Michael . . . Michael . . ." I heard a man's voice.

Why do I feel so far away? I couldn't figure out what happened. I wondered how I might get back.

"The doctor wants you to get up, take a shower, and use the bathroom." This time, I heard a woman's voice.

"Yeah, okay," I managed to answer. I was struggling to gather my thoughts. My head was foggy. My eyes were blurry. My hands felt like weights.

Wow. This is bad.

I attempted to get myself up. Every muscle in my body ached. I was able to get on my feet and shuffle to the bathroom. I was so unstable in the shower that I had to sit down.

"I've made it this far. I can't stop now!" I cried out to God. We were not on good terms. I had always needed Him. Right then, I knew I needed Him like never before.

"Your ride is here!" A voice yelled at the bathroom door.

I had spent the last hour showering and pleading with God, but time was up. My dad had come to take me back to the hotel. I surely did not want him to see me like this. Again.

My mind began to dredge up anxious thoughts. *What if I never get over this? What if I die a hopeless drug addict?*

A nurse came to help me into a wheelchair. My shaky legs wouldn't carry me on my own. She wheeled me to the exit where my dad was waiting. The two of them got me into Dad's car. Dad drove back to the same hotel where I had stayed last night. We checked in. Dad helped me shuffle to the room and settled me into the bed. I was exhausted and needed to sleep.

A few hours later, my eyes opened wide.

Where am I?

Slowly, reality set in. It was not a nightmare. It all actually happened.

"How are you feeling?" My dad was right there.

I looked at him through half-open eyes. I managed to mumble a couple of words, "I'm hungry."

"I can go grab some soup and bread, if you want."

That sounded good. I agreed, though I didn't know if I could eat anything.

"The doctor said he was coming to check on you tonight. I can go out to get some food. Then, we can watch a movie while we wait for him."

"That sounds like a good plan." I wasn't sure I could stay awake through a movie. I *was* sure I was glad my dad was with me. After we ate, we decided to sit by the pool instead of watching television. I needed a cigarette anyway. It had been a grueling twenty-four hours. We waited a few hours for the doctor. The fresh air was just what I needed.

The doctor explained to me how I should expect to feel. He gave details about the procedure and exactly how the medication worked. "We essentially 'scrubbed' your brain and removed all the opiates. We put lemon juice into your muscles to help extract the heroin. Each day that goes by, you will feel better and better."

"I hope so. I feel pretty terrible today. I can't keep food down."

The doctor was with us for about an hour. It was still early in the evening, and I was beginning to feel somewhat better. I wanted to take a walk. I tried to stand up. My dad grabbed my arm. The weakness in my legs was evident when I tried to use them. I was shaky, but I could feel the strength coming back. I put one foot in front of the other.

That's how my whole life had been. I thought back to the more than thirty different facilities: all the detoxes, halfway houses, and rehab facilities I had been through. I made it through each one by keeping my head down and putting one foot in front of the other.

"Do you remember that time we went camping?" Dad was reminiscing too. "I forgot to bring blankets and sleeping bags. It was so cold that we couldn't sleep, so we went to stay in a hotel."

"Yes." Nodding my head, I remembered that trip quite clearly. "That was a great trip."

We continued to recall memories. And past mistakes. We laughed and cried for the next few days. On the third day, the doctor came back to check on me. He said I was doing well and released me to go back home. Back to reality. Dad dropped me off at the airport. We shared heartfelt hugs and goodbyes, then I hopped on the plane and headed back to my wife and my life in Chattanooga.

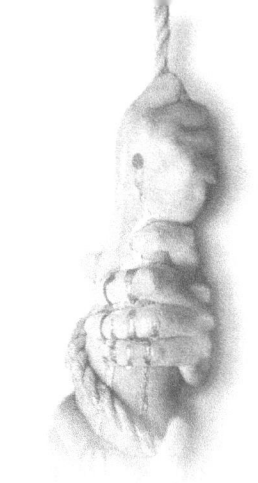

CHAPTER 20

ON THE EDGE

This is my story of redemption, and I wish this chapter began with a promise of sunshine and rainbows. It does not. There are more chapters to be written.

Back home in Chattanooga, I realized how uncomfortable I was in my own skin. I didn't know how to run a successful business. I didn't know how to properly handle relationships. I didn't know how to treat my wife with love and tenderness. I felt like a failure in just about everything. The pain that plagued me daily was unrelenting. The accusing voices would not stay quiet. Having any kind of relationship with God seemed like an unattainable possibility.

Heroin, the voices repeated. *That will be your only relief.* If I was going to continue to be miserable, I might as well be high and numb.

"Hey, man, can I get a gram?" I pressed the button and sent the text. Immediately, the thoughts began running through my mind.

This is going to be really bad. Remember what the doctor said? Your body was reacting badly to detoxing on that gurney. Flopping around like a fish.

My addiction argued back, *Just don't use it for three days straight and you will be fine. You can handle it this time.*

There was that familiar churning in my stomach. I couldn't think straight. The obsession had shown up in earnest. I hurried into my car and sped to the meeting spot. I jumped out and grabbed the plastic baggie with the corner cut. It was twisted into a knot. My hands trembled. Back into the car. I couldn't loosen the knot fast enough. The brown powdery substance spilled out onto the console. The dollar bill rolled up easily. A strong sniff. A sigh of relief. My face grew warm.

There it is. That's what I've been looking for.

Relief was instant, as I knew it would be. The daily emotional turmoil was more than I could bear. This always proved to be the consistent rescue. Sure, it brought a lot of heartache.

Who cares?

The vicious cycle had begun . . . again. Once I started, I couldn't control myself. A few days later, I revisited the dealer. More heroin. High again.

I couldn't hide it from Ivette. She had seen this all before. She could see it in my eyes. "This time, I'm going to stay with my family in Florida if you refuse to get help." She wasn't kidding.

I was afraid my body couldn't handle the pain of detoxing again. I didn't even want to try. Now, I had no choice. I realized the pain of losing my wife would be far greater than the detox experience. Defeated, I made the call. Rapid Detox. Again. The doctor agreed to do it. Again.

Well, here we go.

Ivette and I decided to drive back to South Florida this time. It was the same excruciating experience all over again. The extreme loneliness. The cold hospital. The Valium. And, yes, the diaper.

Why do I keep doing this to myself?

After the procedure, the doctor came into the room to check on me. "I can never take you as a patient for this procedure again. We almost lost you twice while you were under anesthesia." He raised his eyebrows. He exhaled a long, slow breath. Turning to Ivette, he declared, "If he tries another Rapid Detox, they'll be taking him out in a body bag."

My wife couldn't disguise her deep concern. I was profoundly affected by the doctor's words, but exhaustion kept me from seriously processing them.

Ivette was able to help me slide into the passenger seat. We left the hospital in silence. I believe that may have been the longest car ride I have ever endured. We had to pick up Naltrexone, an opiate blocker, at the pharmacy before heading back to the hotel. It essentially blocks the receptors in the brain, so opiates won't work. I would be unable to get high.

It took all of my resolve to get myself out of the car at the hotel. Ivette put her arm around me, and I rested my weight on her shoulders. She had become the perfect example of love and acceptance. She had become my rock.

Words began to form in my mind. *Lord, help me to overcome.*

Other, more familiar voices screamed louder. *You will never be good enough. You are a drug addict. A loser. You will die that way.*

I collapsed onto the bed. Sleep was a welcome refuge from the revelation of the depravity I found myself in.

The next morning came way too fast. Physically, I felt better. Each day, I felt better and better. But the emotional pain stubbornly maintained its power. The doctor came to check on me on the third day. He said I was doing great, so he released me to return home. Back to reality. Again. We packed up the car and set the GPS for Chattanooga. Time doesn't stop for anyone.

Work and responsibilities were impatiently awaiting our arrival. But shame still handicapped me. The accusing voices were obsessive and loud.

You are a loser. You will lose everyone who ever loved and cared for you.

A few months later, I had come up with the perfect plan. If I tried timing the Naltrexone, I might still be able to get high. But I would have to do it just right. Getting high would silence the annoying voices, and maybe I wouldn't get sick from the heroin.

I grabbed the phone and made the call. The same dealer was still in business. He answered before the end of the first ring. I guess he knew I'd be back. I was sure this was the way out. The familiar pain agreed. Even a moment's relief was worth the try. I bought one gram of heroin. It was slightly pink. I knew that meant it was mixed with Fentanyl. I didn't care. I would just use a little less.

My nostril burned as I snorted the powder. I waited. Nothing. The Naltrexone had worked. A few hours later, I tried again. Nothing. That didn't stop me. I kept trying for forty-eight hours. Finally, warmth flushed my face. I'm sure my pupils had turned into pinpoints.

I think I figured it out.

Over the next few weeks, I kept trying. There was no science to it. I decided I needed to stop taking the Naltrexone. I kept snorting the heroin. It would be hard to fool Ivette. She would notice the telltale fact that my pupils were small. But I knew that cocaine makes the pupils dilate.

Good idea.

I would smoke crack after work. That way, I wouldn't get caught. It had the opposite effect. Once I took the first hit of crack, I couldn't stop. My desire to stop using drugs was enormous and very real. But even still, thinking about being hit with the full force of the shame and disappointment in myself was considerably more convincing. I had to keep the voices quiet. Stored-up thoughts from years back plagued me.

Wouldn't it be cool to get a thousand dollars' worth of crack and just smoke until I couldn't anymore? To blow out and disappear? To crawl in a hole and forget about this existence?

That was dangerous thinking. I could not do that. Ivette loved me so much. I could not break her heart that way. We had a business and a life beyond our wildest dreams. I wondered if these things were none other than blessings given to us by God. In spite of myself, a tiny ray of hope grew in my soul. I truly wanted to believe that somehow I could be healed, that this obsession would be taken from me and I would be free. I had been to so many rehab programs where I had received counsel from numerous therapists. I had heard my dad preach countless sermons. The idea that God loved me and held me safely in His hands was an idea that had stalked me my whole life. It was only God Who could have kept me alive through so many harrowing circumstances where I might have died.

I should have died.

I was sure it was He Who held me back now.

CHAPTER 21

BLUE SKIES AHEAD

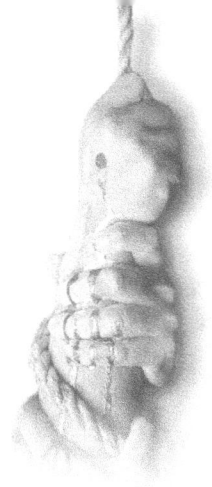

"Babe, we need to go away for a few days. I desperately want to stop using drugs."

"Let's go." My wife didn't hesitate. "Let's go to Gatlinburg. We've been wanting to go there."

How did she remain so peaceful? I took time off from work. We packed a bag and left. Ivette didn't know that I still had a gram of heroin. I planned to throw it away, but I couldn't. The fear of being sick gripped me. I was riddled with anxiety. We drove to the hotel and settled in.

"Let's go explore and find a good place to eat." Ivette was looking forward to having a fun time together, away from all the demands of our business.

I was happy, too. I had enough heroin to last me a week.

I can just duck and hide and stay high this whole time. That was a bad thought. I tried to fight it, but I still went into restrooms every chance I got. I continued using and hiding. We went on rides, and we played mini-golf. We toured antique shops. We went to a restaurant to eat. I was continuing to get high. I knew I would have to stop.

"Can we go back to the hotel to rest and freshen up?" Ivette was getting tired.

As we headed back to the hotel, desperation was growing inside me. I knew it was time to decide. I had to throw the heroin away, or I would never stop. The fear of getting sick was weighing heavily on my mind. I could barely think reasonable thoughts. It felt like the little devil on one shoulder and the little angel on the other were screaming at me. However, this time, it was life and death fighting for my attention. Shame and guilt crushed my heart. I was such a fake. The disappointment I had caused my loved ones throughout the years played over and over in my mind. Ivette still had no idea what was going on.

I can't tell her. I can't disappoint her again.

When we got to the room, Ivette told me she was going to take our dog, Ella, for a walk. I knew this was my moment. I went into the bathroom and closed the door. I held the bag of heroin.

"Lord, I need You. Please help me." That was the most sincere prayer I had ever prayed.

I opened the baggie and watched the powder slip into the toilet. I washed out the baggie to make sure all the residue was gone. As I went outside to be with Ivette and Ella, I put the baggie in the trash bin by the outside door. That was it.

I will surely be sick in a couple of hours. I had to keep moving. I couldn't ruin yet another day for my wife.

After resting for a while, I still didn't feel any effects. "Hey, babe, let's find a nice place for dinner."

I was trying to stay positive. I had detoxed without medicine before, although it was nearly impossible for me. The cure for being dope sick is easy: take more opiates. They're always just a phone call away. There were moments when I had done anything to take away the sickness—and I mean anything. I have sold my soul. I have compounded my shame to depths I'm embarrassed to think about or mention. If you can think of it, I probably have done it just to get high. I was sure this time would be no different. The fear and expectation were insufferable. I did my best to keep a poker face. I had to do it for Ivette.

Lord, help me!

I finally decided I would have to tell Ivette something. I would downplay it. If I did get badly ill, she deserved to know what was happening. After dinner, we went back to the hotel. I crawled into the bed. I wasn't sick. I just knew what was coming. The mornings were always the worst.

"Goodnight, babe." My voice sounded a little sad. "I love you."

She put her arm around me and stayed close to me as we dozed off. She whispered back, "I love you, too. I will never stop believing that the Lord will give me my miracle and heal you."

I closed my eyes and drifted off to sleep. I didn't dream that night, and I didn't wake up. Not once. I slept like a baby. In the morning, I woke up, but I dreaded opening my eyes. Amazingly, my body was not in pain. I didn't feel sick, but I just knew, if I opened my eyes, it would hit me. I tried to go back to sleep. I didn't want to face what was coming. I realized I was feeling hungry. That was very unusual.

I never get hungry when I'm dope sick.

"Good morning, babe." I didn't trust my voice for more than a whisper. "Let's go get breakfast."

We dressed and headed out for another adventurous day. The thoughts of the impending sickness plagued me. I decided to just keep going until I had to deal with it. We had a pretty amazing breakfast. The food tasted so good.

Maybe it will take twenty-four hours. It's sure to hit me before bed tonight.

Ivette and I enjoyed a day filled with laughter and excitement. We rode a roller coaster. We ate incredible food. It was a day I will always remember.

Evening came. Still nothing. No sickness ever came over me. I was shocked. *Am I healed?* I was plagued with doubt, but no sickness. That night, I slept better than the night before. Another morning came. No shakes. No cold sweats. No excruciating pain. No immense regret.

"Babe, I think God must have healed me. I haven't been sick." I had to tell her the whole truth.

We both thanked God for this miracle He was doing in my life. I had spent more than twenty years struggling with addiction. I spent too much time believing that I didn't deserve anything good in my life. I had felt rejected, abandoned, and so alone. I had learned to push people away before they had a chance to leave on their own. Many, many times I wished to just die. I wished the drugs would put me to sleep and I would never wake up. I was bound by the difficulties of my past. I was forever searching for temporary relief that would only cause further harm.

But was I really free?

I wasn't quite done. We had been in Gatlinburg for five meaningful days, and that time was coming to a close. We had to return to real life. We packed up and started back. With every mile, the discomfort grew. We would have to face the grind of life that had caused me so much pain and suffering.

I don't think I can do this. Familiar voices rose up in my mind. That's right: those voices.

You're no good.

You will never overcome this.

You will always be an addict.

I felt my shoulders slump. Fighting seemed hard. Even with the evidence, I couldn't believe I was truly healed. My lack of sickness was just a fluke.

I should go get high again. This will be way too hard. I need to be numb.

When we arrived home, I made the call. "Yeah, let me get a gram."

It was like watching myself from afar. I drove to the dealer's house wondering what in the world I was doing. I grabbed the baggie and jumped back into the car. I rolled up the dollar bill. The pink and white powder spread onto the console.

This could kill me.

I snorted anyway. Burned my nostril. I didn't care. Suddenly, a blanket of disgust washed over me.

You believed that the Lord healed you from being sick. Are you intent on testing Him now?

"No!" I cried out loud. "Lord, help me!"

I stopped at the very next gas station. The red neon sign that seemed to be taunting me now flashed in my face as if to say I had to stop. I watched the powder slowly dissolve in a cup of water. Joy? Relief. Surrender. I couldn't get it into the trash soon enough. It was over. Miracles do happen.

As sure as the sky is blue. I knew it was over. I knew I was done.

CHAPTER 22

REINVENTED

The next morning, I woke up thinking everything should and would be different. But everything wasn't. Regardless of what happens to us, life still moves on. The pain was still there. However, I could tell that the obsession for continuing to use drugs was gone. All the trauma, and its residue, were not. Like always, the feelings of rejection, abandonment, loneliness, anger, of being no good, and of being a failure were still agonizingly present. The familiar emotions were plaguing me. I had no idea what to do.

My only thought was . . . *Jesus!*

I called out to Him, begging His attention. If Jesus could rescue me from the enormous monster the addiction had become, He could definitely heal the pain and the trauma. He was with me in this battle. I leaned in. I had to fight. I would stand up, face my enemies, and fight. I would not give up.

Over the years, I had spoken with many counselors: pastors, peer counselors, mental health counselors, biblical counselors, and recovery support counselors. I was not convinced that any of them could really help me. Ivette had been encouraging me to try counseling again. This time, I was ready. Through a series of events I believe only God could have orchestrated, we found someone to help us. This counselor was amazing. We got together and went to work.

I had wanted God to just snap His fingers and fix me all at once. Though He is certainly able, He rarely works that way. I had no idea how much help I needed until I began to receive it. Living life as a drug addict for so many years keeps someone from properly learning how to function as a responsible adult, make wise decisions, manage stress successfully, solve problems effectively, and have a healthy view of themselves as a person. It was going to be a long road back. But I was excited and motivated to put in the effort.

We had intentionally chosen a counselor who had a biblical perspective. As time went on, I began to understand more clearly Who God is and who I am as His creation. Slowly and cautiously, I was able to look at the painful trauma of losing my mother at such a young age. I was able to examine the emotions that held me hostage for so long and work on becoming untangled from their power. My life was developing into a safer and more comfortable place to be.

The love I had for my incredible wife grew to new heights. I began to see our marriage more from God's point of view, with His value and purpose. I was reading and studying the Bible daily. Ivette and I were staying connected to other Christians who supported and encouraged us. As I began to heal and become more whole and more healthy, life began to change for us in amazing ways.

I believe I was (and am) being reinvented. "Reinvent" is defined as "to completely change something so thoroughly that it seems brand new" (Vocabulary.com, s.v. "reinvent," accessed February 17, 2024, https://www.vocabulary.com/dictionary/reinvent.). The reason we named our company "Reinvented Concepts" was because of something I felt God had allowed me to experience back in 2006.

I was staying at a Teen Challenge rehab facility at the time. One day, I was sitting in the chapel watching a worship band's music video. The camera panned out and I spied a young girl in the audience who appeared to be caught up in the worship. At that moment, I had what seemed like a vision of myself on the stage, looking at her. It was as if I could see her wandering heart being drawn back to God, the One Who loved her. I knew I was God's original "invention." I sensed Him assuring me that He could, and would, reinvent me and reinvent my life. I had read in the Bible that all things, including me, could become new. It was a promise I needed to hold on to. Now, I could see it unfolding. I had hope that I could become the person God had created me to be.

Ivette and I have made our share of mistakes. We've lost money on unwise business deals. There were times when we were pretty deep in debt. I had taken some risks that didn't work as I had hoped.

One day, Ivette, my dad, and I were headed to a restaurant when I received a phone call from someone I hadn't spoken to in at least three years.

"Hey, Mike." As we exchanged polite greetings, I wondered why this guy would be calling me now. "I'm the new operations manager at a company that sells gutter protection systems. Would you consider becoming a Chattanooga sales rep for me?"

Hesitation. Apprehension. Doubt. Fear of the unknown. I experienced a range of emotions.

Could I be good at this? What if God was behind this opportunity?

"Yes. I'll take the job."

That became one of the most important decisions of my life. I determined I would give it my best efforts. As the saying goes, "Bloom where you are planted." I had learned that motto years ago at a rehab facility and kept it in the back of my mind ever since. I have used it successfully on many occasions. I implemented it in this job and I have consistently been one of the top salesmen in the office. This job gave us the income we needed to keep going—far beyond what we could have imagined. It especially benefitted us during the COVID-19 shutdowns when Ivette was laid off from her job. In addition, the job helped me to grow and mature emotionally. Learning to meet and communicate with new people every day challenged me to continually strive to be at my best.

The reality is that whether we are having our best day or our worst day, we still have to face this thing called life. Emotions are a part of it, both the positive and the negative ones. The obsession to use drugs no longer haunted me. I would have to continue to manage the emotions. I had discovered that feelings would always tell you lies, but I had also discovered that, standing on the truth, your feelings can be restrained, controlled, or overcome.

Recently, I went to bed angry. I was angry because I felt like my wife had neglected me. I was sharply aware of what was happening. I was powerless to stop the process. I was that eleven-year-old boy again, hiding under the bed, convinced that I didn't matter and I never would. I recognized the pain that began as a knot in the back of my throat. Like black, bony hands with razor-sharp nails, it reached out from the darkness and clutched at my throat, my body, and my mind. This experience was not unfamiliar. Like so many other nights in the past, shame and condemnation hovered over me. From the darkness, accusing voices reminded me of my failures and my worthless attempts to be free and live a normal life.

There is no hope for you. You were born to be a drug addict. You think God could love you?

I couldn't move. I was paralyzed, trapped in the darkness with my enemies.

Unexpectedly, a new kind of anger began to emerge—anger *at* those enemies. Anger at the addiction that had taken away so much of my life. Anger that gave me the strength to fight back. I would refuse to believe those lies. I would declare the truth. In the past, I would have called my dealer. Drugs would rescue me. This incident would have been the beginning of a days-long drug binge. This time, I made a different call. I called out the name of the only One I knew was on my side. The One I knew wanted me to win.

Jesus!

I had been scheduled to lead a Bible study the next morning. I had gone to bed pretty sure I had nothing to offer. After battling my enemies in the night, I felt like God had awakened me with plenty to say. Encouraging others from the midst of your own sufferings is especially effective.

Some time back, a friend had challenged me to read the Bible every morning and text him my response to the words I read. I did it. If I'm being honest, I did it more out of spite than desire.

Huh. You have nothing on me. I can do this.

I did it for close to five months. Most mornings, I read the Bible while I was high on Fentanyl or heroin. Despite my rebellious attitude, the Word of God had gotten into me, into my heart and my soul. His powerful words were hiding in my heart. I guess my friend knew those words would one day be fruitful. And they have been. They gave me the strength I needed to surrender.

Surrender was only the first step. A complete return to health and wholeness will likely take the rest of my life. The abuse of drugs and other substances is a serious and complex disorder. It has been, and still is being, extensively studied to determine the causes, effects, and most beneficial treatments.

I know that all day, every day, I will need to remain vigilant. Always learning. Always being committed to recovery. Always depending on God, Who created me and Who is my refuge and my help. I remember my mom often encouraging me with this phrase: "Hard work and perseverance bring reward!"

How true it is. One step at a time. One day at a time.

If a cemetery could be described as quaint, Prosper Cemetery, sitting in a small meadow off a dirt road in Woodstock, Vermont, would be it. A group of large hardwood trees stand guard near the entrance. A length of chain connected to two poles pretends to be a gate. Around forty family members and friends were gathered there to participate in a unique event.

My mother is buried in Florida where we lived when she died. Her mother, my grandmother, who lived in Vermont where mom grew up, rarely visited Florida. Grammy was always a little sad that she couldn't often visit Mom's gravesite. So, in 2019, Mom's two sisters, my Aunt Kathy and her sister, my Aunt Nancy, designed a ceremony that would symbolically "reunite" my mother and her mother.

Grammy died in 2011 and was buried at Prosper Cemetery beside her husband, my mother's father. I never knew him, as he passed away before I was born. If you toured the headstones, you would discover that many of my family's ancestors have been buried there since the 1800s.

My mom's brother handcrafted a beautiful cedar memory box, lined with red velvet. It sat on a purple scarf upon its burial place above Grammy's grave. Mom's graduation picture had been placed near the box, surrounded by bright flowers. Irises, Mom's favorite, took center stage in the display. During the service, the lovely box was filled with cards, pictures, and mementos. Several of the attendees shared stories and memories of Mom.

I was comforted by the obvious place of esteem she held in the hearts of so many loved ones.

I had not attended my mother's funeral or burial. As an adult, this was a weighty event for me. I recognized it as an opportunity to begin a journey of restoration and healing. I needed to allow the deep wounds inflicted by losing my mother when I was so young to be soothed and mended. I would forever be affected by her death. But more than that, I desired to remain more affected by her life. I placed mementos into the box. I spoke of my love and admiration for the remarkable woman who gave me life. For a fleeting moment, I was six years old staring into that casket, convinced I could never say goodbye. Say goodbye, I must. Tears were shed as my uncle gently closed and latched the box, removed the purple scarf, and lowered it into the ground.

I glanced at the beautiful, peaceful face looking back from the photograph. Standing there in that quaint Vermont cemetery, surrounded by loved ones who had cheered me on, I sensed this was the beginning of a new chapter, a better life, a road to healing. Leaning over the box, I let my heart release my mother into the arms of Jesus.

I'm looking forward to seeing you again, Mom!

Once again, it was a bright summer day in June.

EPILOGUE

I wrote the last chapter of this book while lying on a lounge chair beside the pool in beautiful Cancun, Mexico, with my lovely wife relaxing on a chair next to me. I'm not boasting about my vacation. Instead, I am celebrating my freedom—freedom from the bondage of drugs that prevented me from enjoying life this way for so many years. Freedom to be in my right mind. To savor the smell of the salty ocean. To be calmed by the sounds of the repeating waves. To want nothing more right now than this peaceful bliss.

At the writing of this book, we are still operating Reinvented Concepts. We own several properties which we rent both short and long–term. Ivette and I are partners in the business. I also continue to be employed in sales. We are abundantly blessed and happy. Our marriage is solid. We are both dedicated to serving the Lord and His people.

Drugs took more than twenty years of my life. As hard as this book about my life may have sounded, I left out most of the worst parts. In order to write it, I had to dredge up every detail of my pain and trauma. I spent two and a half years penning these pages. I revisited relationships and circumstances that contributed to my emotional turmoil. I had to take breaks, and talk to my wife and therapist about what was happening inside of me. Some of the memories were too painful to write. Healing comes at a great cost.

It is vital to remember that healing is a process. It's a process that will seem like it is taking way too long. I sincerely want to be, and stay, clean—drug-free—for the rest of my life. Some of the drugs I was addicted to, and which most addicts choose, disrupt the communication between our brains and our bodies. The capacity to think, plan, make decisions, solve problems, and use self-control is altered. A twenty-eight-day rehabilitation program will not fix this. Long-term help is required. But recovery is possible. Staying clean for longer periods gives the brain time to heal. If you find yourself in a place where you need healing, know this—when you are willing to endure the process, you will reap great rewards.

Life happens daily! Despite the internal battle going on, I have to fix flat tires, go to work, repair broken toilets, go to church, spend time with my wife and family members, and work on building relationships. I am committed to healing. I refuse to give up. Go big or go home, right? I spend time with counselors, mentors, and people who love me and in whom I can trust. Sometimes, I wake up feeling sad and vulnerable, seemingly without cause. Some days, the weight of life seems too heavy to handle. Yet I know there is a better way to live.

I believe with all my heart that true healing, healing of all aspects of life, comes when we turn our lives over to Jesus Christ, the Son of God. He is real. He is present. He loves us. He forgives us for everything—every sin. He knows all about our suffering. He sees us in our darkest moments. He sees us at our lowest places. Still, He loves us without restraint. He is the One Who is able, and wants to, heal us. He desires to see us whole and healthy here on earth.

All through the pages of this book, through the pages of my life, God has shown up. He never gave up on me. I am learning to look for Him and to lean on Him every day. Many days, I am on my knees calling out, "Where are You, God?" The Bible tells me that He will fight for me. When my own weakness stops me,

His strength keeps me going. When I am weary from this battle, I can run to Him to find rest.

Reader, these words are for you!

If you have picked up this book, you are likely an addict or you love someone who is an addict.

If you are an addict, if you are high right now, go get help. **Right now!** Don't wait. Let this desperation you are feeling be the catalyst that drives you to a path of healing. No more excuses. Don't promise yourself you will stop. Don't let pride shame you. Admit you need help and go after it. It will take time. We will be in the healing process until we die. But we *have to begin* the process. I know all the excuses. I've used them all.

If you love someone who is an addict, be encouraged. Don't give up on them. Don't enable them by providing money or rides. Give them love. Learn all you can about them and why they are suffering. Have ready a list of detox and rehab facilities you could help them get into. Help them to locate recovery meetings they can attend.

Drugs and alcohol are not the only addictions people can deal with. If you think you may be addicted or struggle with an eating disorder, pornography, body dysmorphia, gambling, worry, anger, or anything I have not mentioned, you need to seek help. If you have been trying to overcome it in your own strength and have failed, you need to seek help. Find a trusted friend, mentor, counselor, pastor, or therapist and get started on recovery.

I wrote this book for you because I get you. I can relate to the pain you have felt and continue to experience. I believe God is for you. He is saying to each of us, "Come to Me all of you who are tired from the heavy burden you have been forced to carry. I will give you rest" (Matt. 11:28 ERV). I want you to know you **can** live a new and better life—better than anything you may have ever imagined.

I encourage you to say *Yes!* to Jesus. He wants you to be His. Say *Yes!* today.

Dear Jesus, I believe You are God's Son. I believe You died and rose from the dead to pay for my sins. Help me overcome my doubt. I ask You to fill me with Your love. Begin healing me from the inside out. I give You my heart and my life.

Amen.

ACKNOWLEDGMENTS

The following people are the reasons I am alive today.

My precious wife, Ivette Cinelli. Thank you, Ivette, for seeking the Lord with fervor, praying without ceasing, and loving me with boundless love. You are the strongest, most faith-filled woman I have ever known. The Lord must have put something special in your heart for me. So many times, even in my most shameful condition, you held my hands, looked me in the eyes, and said, "I am here and I am not leaving. What do we need to do to get help for you?" You never stopped believing for your miracle. You are forever the love of my life.

My dad, Mario Cinelli. My dad and I are still the best of friends. Thank you, Dad, for never giving up and always showing up. You are a man committed to God above all else. You are my example of the true love of God. I hurt you the most, yet you stood by me at my very worst. You have been my reason for enduring the fight. You will always be my best friend.

My stepmom, Cherie Cinelli. Thank you for being a stepmother any child would be fortunate to have. You have shown me what commitment and perseverance really mean. Thank you for taking care of my dad and of me. I love you. Your love and support for me will never be forgotten, and I am grateful we continue to grow closer.

My aunt, Kathleen Sutton. Aunt Kathy is still very present in my life. In fact, she now works as my bookkeeper. Thank you, Auntie Kathy, for being my hero. You have taught me many life lessons just by the way you live your life. You accepted me into your home, offered help, and never rejected me. I always knew you would be there if I needed you. I appreciate you and love you forever.

My mom, Debbie Cinelli. Thank you, Mom, for the prayers you prayed over me, even as an infant. Your love for Jesus was imparted to me. You were an amazing mother. I am sorry we had to be separated so soon, but I will persevere in your honor.

And thank you to the countless people, most of whom I do not even know, who spent time praying for me and for my family for so many years.

GOODBYE

Goodbye, my love; my only friend
Comfort in wondrous chaos to the end
To cuddle in misery, thirsting for more
A passion for death, regret to live for
Happiness once tangible, dissipating to memories
Finding solace in the most burden, the cycle for centuries
The needle set how my life was lived the easy way out
A shameful legacy to leave, no doubt
To overcome greatly overwhelms, to bury is pain
Life a fierce battle, with little or no gain
Drugs cause uncontrollable tears
Grabbing my soul and ruining the years
No use in pursuing a purpose or meaning
Security found in hands of eternal grieving
Heroin is those hands, held on so tight
Begging for release, not putting up a fight
Searching for truth, summons the past
Face all those burdens, release them at last
God has control of my pain and my hurt
I'm sorry dear friend, I can't even flirt
God has taken the desire; His love He'll send
Goodbye, to you; no longer my friend.

ABOUT THE AUTHOR

Mike Cinelli loves the thrill of pulling all the pieces together to make a good deal. For him, a good deal is the one where the buyer and the seller both come out as winners.

Mike is a stouthearted entrepreneur and businessman, but it hasn't always been that way. Having spent twenty years of his life struggling with a heroin and crack cocaine addiction, he has suffered the consequences of repeatedly making wrong choices.

One day, a transformational encounter with Jesus Christ made all the broken pieces of his life fall into place. He agreed to the one covenant that gave his life new meaning and purpose. Mike is firmly convinced that surrendering your life to Jesus is the only way to escape the pain and oppression of drug addiction for good.

Driven by a passion for helping others find hope and healing, his deepest desire is to connect people with the God Who loves them and wants them all to be winners in life. Mike has been a friend, a speaker, and a mentor within the recovery community for several years, and has shared his powerful testimony at churches and recovery meetings.

Alongside his other roles, Mike is also a financial coach. Together with other landlords and local businessmen, he speaks, leads workshops, and teaches classes to help others become financially healthy.

Through his book *Reinvented*, Mike hopes to reach people who have been, or are being, affected by addiction with the message that recovery and permanent healing are possible. You can be redeemed and live a better life.

You can find out more about Mike at his website: mikecinelli.com.